W

Also available from CILT:

The Guide to languages and careers: How to continue your languages into Further and Higher Education (2nd edition)

by Ann King with Gareth Thomas

The Centre for Information on Language Teaching and Research provides a complete range of services for language professionals in every stage and sector of education, and in business, in support of its brief to promote Britain's foreign language capability.

CILT is a registered charity, supported by Central Government grants. CILT is based in Covent Garden, London, and its services are delivered through a national collaborative network of regional Comenius Centres in England, the National Comenius Centre of Wales, Scottish CILT and Northern Ireland CILT.

Aiming
high 2

Straight A's

Edited by
Glenis Shaw

with contributions from

Glenis Shaw, Tony Lonsdale, Anneli
McLachlan, Ann Barnes, Sheila Barbour,
Hilary Barker and Keith Marshall

The views expressed in this publication are the contributors' and do not necessarily represent those of CILT.

First published in 2000 by the Centre for Information on Language Teaching and Research, 20 Bedfordbury, Covent Garden, London WC2N 4LB

Copyright © 2000 Centre for Information on Language Teaching and Research

ISBN 1 902031 38 5

2004 2003 2002 2001 2000 / 10 9 8 7 6 5 4 3 2 1

A catalogue record for this book is available from the British Library

Printed in Great Britain by Copyprint (UK) Ltd

The right of Glenis Shaw, Tony Lonsdale, Anneli McLachlan, Ann Barnes, Sheila Barbour, Hilary Barker and Keith Marshall to be identified as authors of this work has been asserted by them in accordance with the Copyright, Designs and Patents Act, 1988.

CILT Publications are available from: **Grantham Book Services**, Isaac Newton Way, Alma Park Industrial Estate, Grantham, Lincs, NG31 8SD. Tel. 01476 541080. Fax: 01476 541061. Book trade representation (UK and Ireland): **Broadcast Book Services**, 2nd Floor, 248 Lavender Hill, London, SW11 1JL. Tel: 020 7924 5615. Fax: 020 7924 2165.

Contents

The contributors

Glenis Shaw
Language Teaching Adviser, CILT

Tony Lonsdale
Vice Principal, Cardinal Newman 6th Form College, Preston

Anneli McLachlan
Head of Modern Foreign Languages, Elliott School, Putney

Ann Barnes
Lecturer in Modern Foreign Languages (teacher education)
University of Warwick

Sheila Barbour
Lecturer, Middlesex University

Hilary Barker
Head of Modern Foreign Languages, St Paul's Girls' School, London

Keith Marshall
Lecturer in Modern Foreign Languages (teacher education)
University of Wales, Bangor

Introduction

Straight A's

Glenis Shaw

Straight A's, the CILT 'A' level show, which took place in July 1998, was 'straight' because it dealt only with 'AS' and 'A' level courses and because of the use of this phrase to denote high achievement in the public examinations. The underlying theme of the conference was indeed about raising achievement and the various strategies in both teaching and learning that lead to students achieving their potential.

Behind the scenes, and following the recommendations of the Dearing report, changes to post-16 accreditation were in progress. A preview of these changes was discussed at the conference. In the meantime QCA has issued a guide to the changes resulting from the consultations for 'Qualifying for success' and 'Qualifications 16–19', outlining the qualifications reforms for education post-16. Changes to 'AS' and 'A' level are quite radical, as outlined in the Epilogue (p77). Teaching for the new examinations will begin in September 2000. The Subject Criteria for Modern Foreign Languages at 'AS' and 'A' level were issued in late June 1999. The three Examination Boards, OCR, Edexcel and AQA, had already submitted draft criteria for the new 'AS' and 'A' level examinations.

Whatever the changes though, the premise of the 1998 conference was that good teaching on 'AS' and 'A' level courses at the present time would still be good teaching for the new specifications. The government is committed to ensuring 'that the rigour of 'A' level is maintained'. Challenging, interesting and motivating students is always the prime objective of modern foreign language teachers at 'A' level. What it is exactly that challenges, interests and motivates students was one of the questions addressed at the conference.

Another underlying theme of the conference in each of the sessions was that achievement could be raised at 'A' level study if study skills and learning strategies were dealt with as an integral part of all aspects of teaching and learning a modern foreign language.

The link between cultural awareness and developing linguistic skills was also explored. Advanced level study of a foreign language requires greater knowledge of the world around us and especially of those countries where the target language is spoken. Learning about historical, geographical and literary aspects of a target language culture can help students to a better understanding and knowledge about use of the target language. Through comparison students' understanding of their own language can also increase. At the conference it was shown how bringing these elements together raised the achievement of students who were already considered high achievers.

A further theme of the conference was the almost constant refrain of 'building up skills'. This applied to linguistic skills as well as to study skills. The ability to deal with longer pieces of written and spoken text in the target language has to be built up gradually. A sense of progressing in knowledge and ability to use the language fluently and accurately should lead to growing confidence. Strategies for comprehension in reading and listening include cultural as well as linguistic ones.

The theme of building up and building on applies to many of the topics for 'AS' and 'A' level which are initially dealt with at GCSE level. Could they be dealt with in greater detail in preparation for further study? How can the teacher build on pre-'A' level knowledge in a more mature and different way? Dealing with topics can be through a range of media – authentic and literary texts, television, cassettes (music or spoken word), the Internet – and can be expressed through oral or written presentations. Drama and role play also have their place.

These were among the issues addressed and discussed at the 1998 conference and which will continue to be of interest to modern languages teachers in the future.

The following chapters were contributed by speakers at the conference. They represent their views and ideas on 'A' level teaching. All of them are practising teachers or trainers.

Chapter 1

Study skills for 'A' level language learners

Tony Lonsdale

A key aspect of the transition from GCSE to 'A' level language learning is that of study skills. All teachers, I am sure, give some attention to raising awareness in their students of the need to take more responsibility for their own learning, but there would seem to be few resources, materials or guidelines that can support teachers and learners in practical ways to develop quickly and effectively sound study skills and study habits. In this paper I wish to outline some practical strategies to achieve precisely that organised and well-managed approach to independent learning that can help confident and competent language users and communicators to become confident and competent language learners and linguists.

Study skills for language learners are a quite specific set of skills, competences and practices, and 'A' level language teachers are not always supported in their efforts to encourage these by the perceptions students bring with them from their GCSE experience. Past experience will tend, by and large, to raise quite the wrong expectations in learners. GCSE achievers may well embark upon 'A' level believing the following to be true:

- that simply being in lessons leads to effective learning and to eventual examination success,
- that the teacher knows from a detailed, prescriptive syllabus what the learner needs to know and will deliver accordingly;
- that everything can be revised for and everything has its list.

Nor will the experience of other 'A' level subjects necessarily assist students in understanding the quite specific nature of 'A' level language study skills. Many subjects are content-based, and the syllabus can be quantified and defined in terms of 'set' topics and knowledge-based units of learning. Students will compile files of facts and information which will inform their essay-writing. They will encounter clearly prescribed units of work which can be checked off as done and completed, and which can then be built into a planned revision programme. Language syllabuses, for the most part, do not follow this pattern. Topics and themes are a vehicle for developing skills, a means to an end rather than an end in themselves.

In helping students to acquire study skills for language learning, therefore, we need to be quite certain about the specific skills language learners need. I have listed below what I see these 'priority skills' to be:

- **Time-management**: what to do when and how much, how often; how to balance time over the skills to be developed and practised.
- **Managing their own learning**: understanding the relationship between contact-time (starting-points) and private study (follow-up and extension work).
- **Effective management of learning resources**: dictionaries; audio/video cassettes; reading materials – how to use these productively.
- **How to prepare set assignments and how to follow up corrected assignments**: learning from mistakes and errors.
- **What is meant by revision and the importance of regular review.**
- **Building one's own learning resources**: organising vocabulary systems; the management of hand-outs and note-taking; managing grammar.
- **Monitoring one's own learning**: trouble-shooting; remedying weaknesses and identifying strengths.

These skills need to be illustrated and practised rather than simply talked about, and I would recommend that they should feature significantly in an induction phase of the 'A' level course, i.e. that there should be a planned study skills focus in the early stages of the first term where **learning by doing** gives emphasis to these skills. I have found it more beneficial to students to 'drip-feed' activities and tasks with a study skills focus over, say, the first half-term rather than to risk overwhelming students with a very intensive package of strategies and techniques for improved learning.

I have set out in the following table a number of **study skills activities, resources** and **approaches** which are relevant to objectives and outcomes in terms of what we are aiming to demonstrate to students as key-aspects of 'A' level language learning. These are 'generic' to language learning and so can be transferred across all languages and can be adapted to any start of course materials and resources, whether that course is a continuation from GCSE or an ab initio course.

?

What we are aiming to demonstrate ...

➡ **Activities, resources and approaches**

?

The scope of an 'A' level language
syllabus ...

➡ **P**repare in English a bullet-point summary of topics/themes covered in a previous year's papers across the full range of questions. Relate this analysis to a copy of the syllabus. What conclusions can be drawn by the group about the diversity of topics and of language being tested? How does the lack of predictability at 'A' level compare with their GCSE experience of language learning? What are the implications in terms of effective 'A' level preparation?

?

The need to maximise contact
with the foreign language ...

➡ **B**rainstorming in English: how different would learning a language be if you were in the target-country? Would it be easier or more difficult? What range of sources of and opportunities for language learning would there be? How would your skills develop? Would some skills develop more than others? What are the implications of this in your present context, i.e. as language learners away from the target-country? This discussion leads logically into the importance of matching contact-time with independent study.

?

How learning contributes to
improved performance in listening ...

➡ **P**lay to students twice a short, off-air listening stimulus. On a two-column response-sheet, students should note in column one words recognised and information understood. They should attempt to write a short summary in English of the item. They should then assess their level of understanding, discussing with partners or in small groups how they think they have performed. The teacher then displays on an OHP a glossary of ten to fifteen key items of vocabulary from the stimulus with meanings in English. Students are given five minutes 'viewing and learning' time. The listening task is then repeated with the same stimulus and this time words and notes are added to column two on the response sheet. Set a summary to be written in English.

Compare the outcomes between the two tasks: has listening comprehension improved? In what ways? What conclusions can be drawn from this about listening performance and about the importance of vocabulary learning and extension?

?

What we are aiming to demonstrate ...

➡ **Activities, resources and approaches**

?

How to access vocabulary from written
sources. How to use a dictionary (1) ...

➡ **A**ctivity one: students work in pairs on a passage of text. Each pair's copy of the text has different words highlighted. The exercise involves finding the highlighted words in the dictionary. Some items will be found as they appear in the text; others will need 'converting'. The teacher circulates and advises where necessary.

Activity two: the teacher displays on OHP the full list of items highlighted with meanings in English, i.e. correct vocabulary listings. Compare this version with how students have noted items and discuss the differences, stressing the importance of effective dictionary usage and vocabulary research for language extension. Language from a reading-source can extend the student's productive language resources. Transfer items to a vocabulary notebook – N.B. a short-term record of language items. Use this approach as the basis for a series of dictionary exercises for homework assignments.

?

Managing vocabulary: noting; sorting;
storing and learning ...

➡ **F**rom the above strategy, develop the idea and the practice of seeing the vocabulary notebook as a short-term record. Encourage students to invest in (or make their own) card index system for vocabulary. On a weekly basis, they will be transferring items from the notebook to the card index system. Discuss strategies for classifying language items within that system. Here are some suggested starting points:

'Headings' for vocabulary cards in the card index system should ideally be generated by the students themselves. Thinking of links and associations is an important part of the vocabulary reviewing and learning process, but students usually need some suggestions and ideas to 'kick start' the process. Suggestions might include:

• theme or topic links (words to do with ...);

• action or movement links (things you do with your eyes; ways of getting places);

• in-the-manner-of-the-word links
(screaming/shouting/whispering etc);

?

What we are aiming to demonstrate ...

➡ **Activities, resources and approaches**

cont'd
- physical features links; general to specific links (doing the housework ... cleaning, cooking, washing-up, etc; thence cleaning ... dusting; polishing; scrubbing; wiping; sweeping, etc);

- pattern of structure links (it's easy / difficult / essential / important / logical to do);

- word-behaviour links (to decide to do; to refuse to do; to try to do, etc)

This weekly, regular task encourages students to review language; to think about how they will classify words and therefore to look at words; to build up a vocabulary resource and in so doing to keep returning to items already noted (thus reinforcing their learning); and to develop a working system of vocabulary management which is more 'user-friendly' and is a more effective learning tool than a notebook.

?

How to use a dictionary (2) and how to make language already acquired work for you ...

➡ **S**elect a passage for translation into English. Set the translation to be done in small groups according to precise instructions:

- read the passage twice to get the general sense of it;

- translate into English all the parts of the passage you are confident you understand;

- fill in a three-column response sheet:
  Column one: identify and write down those words you are not sure about. Review what you have been able to translate and see if that helps you guess the meaning of any 'unknown' words.
  Column two: write down any guesses at the meaning of words. Be as speculative as you need to be, i.e. try to arrive at some interpretation of the words not known;

- 'test' your guess-work by using a dictionary:
  in column three: either tick the guess as an accurate one or write in the proper meaning of the word.

?

What we are aiming to demonstrate ...

➡ **Activities, resources and approaches**

?

Towards thinking in the foreign
language ...

➡ **D**eveloping strategies in written and spoken expression which avoid having immediate recourse to the dictionary to 'convey' an idea formulated in English. Word for word transfer from English to anglicised foreign language is the major obstacle to progress for very many post-GCSE language users.

Structure spoken language tasks so that they progress from concrete, factual 'utterances' to abstract, opinionative ones.

Use plenty of visuals showing people in different contexts. Use 'imagine you are ... and tell me about your life' cues, i.e. work from GCSE personal information starting-points.

Feed into the spoken expression appropriate modelled structures that will develop the learner's range of language.

Set reinforcement exercises with precise constraints and parameters ... ten statements using set structures.

Discipline the students to operate within what they know to be accurate structures and idioms.

Ban the use of dictionaries in spoken and written expression.

?

How to tackle grammar and accuracy
issues ...

➡ **T**he above strategy gives more effective control to 'staged' progression in grammar and range of structures. Students compile a grammar reference of structures and points of language 'presented' by the teacher for communication purposes. These are regularly reinforced and consolidated through 'set menu' exercises and tasks.

As students progress to more extensive writing (short paragraphs; short compositions) and work is corrected, they begin to compile a grammar log book in which they document and record their errors and inaccuracies, their corrections. This then becomes their check-list for inaccuracies.

Teachers can link into this individualised (and differentiated) accuracy target; can prioritise with students 'grammar action points'. Students move at different paces through the challenges of grammar. Adjective agreements may be one student's 'challenge' in a given piece of written work, whereas another student might be ready to get to grips with complex modal verb structures.

The above programme fairly comprehensively sets out the study skills agenda for effective 'A' level language study: it challenges the student to consider how the week's study programme can be organised in order to allocate appropriate amounts of time to the various study tasks. It illustrates very clearly that when a language lesson is over, the work really is only just beginning: contact-time is constantly providing 'parcels of learning', either through review, consolidation, preparation or follow-up. And it is the student's responsibility to grasp these particular nettles and to start organising time effectively.

Here again, the teacher can guide and advise in a very specific way: the direction that I recommend is set out in the **study schedule** below. Students are recommended to organise their private study over the week into five units of one hour: whether these correspond to five weekdays or three weekdays and the weekend depends on the individual and on other commitments. Each one-hour unit is broken down into shorter periods of time that are appropriate to a range of different tasks and skills-practice.

This recommended study schedule is the culminating point in the study skills programme and forms part of a teaching and learning agreement which students are asked to sign as a statement of their commitment. They are then given a series of 'blank' study timetables which they complete as 'actual time-sheets' and have signed off by the teacher on a weekly basis. This is a useful mechanism for both the teacher and the student themselves to monitor their study 'in-put' and forms the basis of review and target-setting in one-to-one progress checks.

Study Schedule

SKILL AREA	DAY 1	DAY 2	DAY 3	DAY 4	DAY 5
Listening	15 mins	15 mins	15 mins	15 mins	15 mins
Vocabulary transfer & learning		15 mins			20 mins
Grammar review	15 mins		15 mins		15 mins
Reading assignment	20 mins		20 mins		
Lesson review	10 mins	10 mins	10 mins	10 mins	10 mins
Preparing set assignments		20 mins		35 mins	
Total	60 mins	60 mins	60 mins	60 mins	60 mins

What I have attempted to provide in the above strategies is a very practical framework of support for teachers to guide students towards effective independent study. In my experience, students welcome this level of guidance and support ... and I very much hope that teachers likewise welcome my contribution to this collection of articles.

Appendix 1: Handbook for Cardinal Newman College

Study skills for modern languages

You have now completed the first half-term of your 'AS' level or 'A' language course and already you will be able to see that language learning post-GCSE covers a wide range of skills, a wide range of subjects and topics, and a very wide range of language. You are moving from a well-defined learning-programme to one that is far more extensive.

'AS' level or 'A' language study requires a different approach to learning. Whereas, previously, the work completed in lessons and homework prepared you to acquire the skills and language tested at GCSE, now there is a need for you to supplement what the lessons and homework assignments provide through your own programme of private study.

This is a new responsibility for you to take on. For your teacher to say 'You should be doing five hours' work a week on each 'A' level language', and leave it at that, would hardly be helpful to you. And that is why this handbook has been produced. It sets out a recommended programme of language learning which deals with all aspects of private study: how you should organise your time to practise and improve the range of skills; how you should organise your learning material; how you should make sure you're keeping to your learning programme. In short, this handbook explains how our contribution to your learning combines with your contribution to make sure that you can now begin to follow a regular programme of language learning which will enable you to make real progress towards meeting the full demands and requirements of 'A' level or 'AS' assessment.

1 Time-tabled lessons: a series of starting-points

One of the key features of effective study and learning is the importance of review. Even when you are fully concentrating on what's happening in the lesson; even when everything in the lesson is absolutely clear; when you're making notes and jotting down points, there is no guarantee that you are learning. Understanding and following what's going on, yes. But actually learning requires you to go over the material again and make the effort to 'fix' those points in your mind, to exercise your memory in order to retain what you have understood. Review and learning are the process by which you make that lesson-material into your stick of knowledge.

That is why the time-tables lessons have to be seen as starting-points in your learning process. Sometimes, the follow-up will be directed and set by the teacher through a homework assignment. But when this is not the case, it is up to you to complete you own follow-up work.

What happens if you neglect this? The language course that you're following is designed rather like a series of building-blocks. The row that's put into place next term will be built on what's been put in place this term, and the third term builds on the second term, and so on. And next week's block will link in with this week's block ... Your lessons-by-lesson review is what puts each block firmly in place for you. Review is the process by which you consolidate your learning.

We can guarantee, now, that there will be a least four earth-tremors in the course of your 'A' level or 'AS' programme: an exam in December of first year; an exam at the end of first year; an exam in January of second year; and the end-of-course public examination, the real 'biggie' on the Richter scale. If you just take the panic-revision approach immediately before those examinations, you're just plastering over the cracks and gaps that weeks of neglect have caused. And the blocks will crumble! If you consolidate your learning lesson-by-lesson, then even when you're right at the epicentre of the tremor, your language skills will withstand the shock.

So don't be a Polyfilla student!

2   *Organising your weekly study-schedule*

Your weekly study-time should match the amount of contact-time you have with the language, i.e. 5 hours for 'A' level; 2.5 hours for 'AS'.

That amount of time has to be organised in such a way that what you are doing 'targets' what is required for achieving an effective handling of all language skills. Because of the range of tasks and activities involved in this, the most effective approach to organising a study-schedule is to plan a programme based on 'short bursts' of practice and learning rather than think in terms of longer periods of study. The brain responds better to three fifteen-minute bursts of vocabulary-learning, for example, than to a forty-five minute 'slot'.

So the weekly five hours needs to be broken down. First, you should organise your time into five one-hour 'units', i.e. in any week you have five study-units. How you spread these over the week is up to you; 4 weekdays + 1 weekend unit; 3 weekdays + 2 weekend units ... this will no doubt vary from week to week depending on other 'commitments', but it is something that you should plan at the start of the week. You therefore establish the plan for the week in question.

Each one-hour 'unit' then needs to be divided into 'short bursts'. The schedule below does that for you and provides you with a weekly study programme.

Skill/Activity	1	2	3	4	5
a. Listening practice	15	15	15	15	15
b. Vocabulary learning	15		15		15
c. Grammar review & learning		15		15	
d. Lesson review	10	10	10	10	10
e. Set assignments		20	20	20	
f. Reading	20				20
TOTAL	60	60	60	60	60

3   Skills and activities: what to do and how to go about it

i   Listening practice

The purpose of this is to practise and develop your listening skills, not to test them. What you understand is what's important. That's why the prompt-sheet that you have for working on listening material is open-ended: it gives general headings for the sort of information you understand rather than specific questions. If your understanding after you've listened to an item is 'patchy'; if what you put down in your notes is 'something about somebody being arrested', or 'something to do with an accident with, I think, fourteen people seriously injured, motorway, early yesterday morning, bad road conditions' ... i.e. if there are uncertainties, if there is vagueness, that doesn't matter. You're not being asked for a detailed summary of the item: you're being asked to document what you understand, as you understand it. After listening to an item four times, you may have a very good idea as to what it's about, or you may only have 'caught' one or two words. Whichever is the case, it's time to move on to another item.

ii   Vocabulary learning

Gaps in vocabulary are one of the major causes of the damage and destruction that result from earth-tremors.

This is how to approach vocabulary-learning effectively.

a In lessons, **always** use your vocabulary notebook to record items of language as and when they are displayed. Don't write words and meanings in the margin of a photocopied sheet. Don't make vocabulary notes on a sheet of file-paper. Use you vocabulary notebook.

b The vocabulary notebook is a short-term record of language items. What you need for you long-term record is a vocabulary card-index system: if you can afford it, you can buy this as a Perspex box + index cards from Menzies, W.H. Smith's or wherever, or you can recycle a Weetabix box (unfortunately we don't have one we made earlier!) and buy just the cards. This is an essential 'support' for effective vocabulary learning.

c Why it's essential is as follows. The task of transferring items from the vocabulary notebook to the card-system on a regular basis forces you to review vocabulary. This isn't just a copying out exercise because your card-system should be 'structured' in such a way that you have to think about the items you're transferring. You therefore need a system of classifying language items, of establishing groups of words or families of words according to links. The groups you create can be based on any associations that you see between words: you can ask for guidance and help on this from your teacher, but to get you started, the sorts of links that you should be considering are, for example:

- theme-links (e.g. words to do with television; with pollution etc)
- action-links (e.g. things you do with your eyes; different ways of getting somewhere)
- in-the-manner-of-the-word links (e.g. voice: speaking quietly; shouting; screaming; whispering etc)
- physical-features links (e.g. looks: ugly; handsome; slim)
- general-to-specific links (e.g. doing the housework: cleaning; cooking; washing up; peeling vegetables etc)
- function links (e.g. stating opinions: I firmly believe that; in my view; I believe it's important that etc)
- pattern-of-structure links (it's ... to do: it's easy to do; it's difficult to do; it's impossible to do etc)

You compile in this way a system of 'heading-cards' to which vocabulary items are transferred, and the exercise of transferring these forces you to look at and to think about words. You will begin to create and find your way about your own system of storing language; reviewing cards with items on them; reading those items; adding to them.

d You are then working with a system from which it is easier to organise your vocabulary learning: the links and associations help you memorise groups of words; handling individual cards with associated items is more effective than trying to learn pages of words from a vocabulary notebook; you can tick cards that you've learnt and mark the point you last reached when you learnt the entries on a card.

e You've devised a system of working with vocabulary that disciplines you to work at vocabulary on a regular basis. You have a number of specific vocabulary-based activities that set you thinking about and reviewing words.

iii Grammar review and learning

Grammar review is the partner-activity to vocabulary-learning, and the two together will improve your handling of all language skills.

What was said previously about building-blocks applies particularly to points and areas of grammar: they need to be fixed firmly in place through review and learning after the lesson so that what is encountered in subsequent lessons can be understood and then built on to what has gone before, again through review and learning.

As you extend and consolidate your understanding, you will also begin to display this acquired language in your writing and speaking: this doesn't happen automatically. It is something you have to make happen, and something only you can make happen.

Grammar review has also to target errors. Learning from corrected work is of crucial importance: analysing mistakes and errors; understanding corrections; learning the points you've overlooked; checking for these in subsequent work … this is where the teacher-student partnership will guide you to identifying priority targets for grammar learning and where you'll be directed to support-materials and activities.

iv Lesson review

Part of this may be covered in [ii] and [iii]: but you should also re-read any material that's been encountered in lesson-time and develop the work in your own way. Set yourself the task of learning a couple of short sentences that give you facts about an issue or express an opinion about an issue; set yourself a short translation exercise on an extract of text; set yourself an analysis-task based on a point of grammar you've reviewed (a tense-analysis; a verb-ending analysis; a gender-analysis). Any one of these will provide the framework you need for an organised and purposeful review activity which encourages you to 'personalise' the material.

v Set assignments

The time scheduled for these has to be managed in a flexible way: preparing a set assignment will involve some of the other skills and activities listed, and therefore you will be transferring the time allocated to these into your set assignment work. A piece of translation requires reading; vocabulary research; and translating. You should collect your vocabulary and transfer it to your index-systems; then learn it; then return to the passage to translate so that the exercise builds in a recall of what you've learnt. Organise you approach to set assignments so that they are a language-learning exercise, not just a 'doing' exercise to get the thing out of the way. Stagger the preparation over two or three sessions rather than leaving it to be done the night before it's handed in.

'Set assignment' doesn't just refer to preparing a piece of work, but also to the follow-up learning the work provides once it has been corrected and returned. You can learn from you mistakes provided you understand why the mistake has been make. You should always review corrected errors and correct versions of pieces of work carefully. Reviewing corrected work is as important as preparing the work in the first place. Assignments are set and corrected to support your language learning.

vi Reading

There are many different reading activities which cover a range of different sources. These activities can be divided into two main types: gist-reading and detailed reading.

Gist reading practice involves 'skimming' a text to get the general sense. It's important that you approach this type of reading in the right way, and that you keep the following points in mind:

- Don't try and understand the meaning of every single word.
- Don't keep interrupting your reading to look up works in a dictionary.
- Skim the text 'positively', i.e. for what you can understand.
- As you apply this technique, you will begin to identify essential words or phrases that you may need to look up to 'unlock' a section of text.
- Mark these by underlining or highlighting and then complete the dictionary research and vocabulary noting as a separate task.

Gist reading and 'skimming' should be used with longer texts. A newspaper or magazine article, for example, or a novel. Choose articles that correspond to your own interests or on subjects that appeal to you. You might, for example, 'skim' all the headlines of a newspaper to begin with to identify something that is of interest to you.

Detailed reading involves a much closer study of a text. Here you are trying to understand and interpret each word and expression, and this is more of a language-building exercise. The purpose is to research and extend your stock of vocabulary and language. You may concentrate on a short article or on a single paragraph of a longer article; you may thumb through a magazine and look at advertisements as a source of detailed reading; you may select a couple of sentences from something you've read in class and explore these more fully. Some points of technique to apply here are:

- Have a dictionary and your vocabulary notebook at the ready.
- Use the dictionary itself as a reading-source, i.e. look at and note examples of different meanings and uses of a word or expression.
- Concentrate on looking at how a sentence is constructed; how the different elements fit together.
- Pay attention to noting useful phrases and expressions to build into your own stock of productive language.
- With advertisements, use the visual clues to support your understanding of the written language. Often this allows you to make sense of the language even if you have not encountered the words before.
- There should always be something 'written on paper' (vocabulary notebook or index system) following a detailed reading assignment.

Your teacher will give further guidance about sources of reading material relevant to your particular language(s).

4   *Monitoring your actual study activities*

Matching contact-time with independent study in the ways described is expected of you, and represents your commitment to the study programme. To help with the monitoring of this, you are required to 'log' each week the time you spend on different skills and activity areas, to complete a sort of study time-sheet. This serves two purposes:

a It provides you with a convenient method of documenting the time you spend on private study.

b It allows your teacher to see at a glance if the matching is being achieved, and where it isn't, if it isn't, to challenge you to explain why not.

Your weekly log-sheet will be checked frequently by your teacher. This is a formal procedure that operates across the department. If there is cause for concern about a particular student's private study performance, action will be taken to deal with that.

5   *The teacher–student agreement*

The recommendations and guidance set out in this booklet have been agreed by the staff in the Languages Department to be good practice for effective language learning for 'A' level and 'AS' students. The booklet is therefore a statement of our expectations. What we are looking for from you, the student, is a commitment to put these recommendations into practice, an undertaking to carry out what is expected of you.

You are therefore asked to accept this undertaking by signing in the space provided below. Your teacher will also sign as an undertaking to support and assist you with your independent language learning by providing further guidance you may need as the course progresses, and by monitoring regularly the work you are doing.

Student's signature _____ Date _____

Teacher's signature _____ Date _____

Chapter 2

Building up oral skills

Anneli McLachlan

Defining the challenge

The challenge at 'A' level, in all skills, is, of course, to take students from GCSE – where, arguably, expression of opinions, reference to different tenses and the ability to deal with the unpredictable, assure grades A–C – to a level where they can 'demonstrate spontaneous development of ideas and amplification of answers, showing mastery of language forms' (AEB) or 'display an impressive range of lexis, structures and idiom, frequently complex with excellent use of abstract language' (Edexcel). This challenge presents itself particularly starkly in oral work, where an A grade at 'A' level demands near fluency. It is, therefore essential to build up confidence, competence, skills and knowledge from the outset, to enable candidates to 'move beyond purely narrative language and function on a more abstract level linguistically, aiming to deploy a wide range of lexis and structures, both in general and as pertinent to the topic.' (Edexcel teacher examiner 'AS'/'A' level training pack)

It is also incumbent on the teacher to share information with candidates from the outset, so that they are clear about their goals, so that they know to move from concrete ideas to abstract ideas, from simple to complex use of language.* The examination boards provide a welcome wealth of materials – mark schemes, handbooks – to which students should have access if they are to gain the grades of which they are capable.

The stage beyond GCSE, therefore, and the work undertaken in the first term of Year 12 is of the utmost importance in forming good habits and empowering students to be able to move on. A caveat must be issued at this point. There is sometimes a tendency to be fixated by grammar at the beginning of an 'A' level course, but, whilst grammar forms an integral part of 'A' level study, teachers must guard against a resultant neglect of oral work and skills. From the outset, an oral approach to topic work should be adopted, so that this particular skill is taught and validated. There is a pervasive myth that oral skills are simply acquired through 'A' level studies. This must be exploded, they can be taught and refined for **all** language learners at all levels.

The start of the autumn term requires that teachers lead their students into the

---

* See Appendix 1, p24 – Top tips for 'A' level

realms of analysis, so that students can move from utterances such as 'I live with my mum and my sister, my parents are divorced. I see my father once a week' (GCSE) to 'I live with my mum and my brother. I consider that society needs to reassess the changing nature of the family unit' ('A' level). This article aims to highlight some pointers to effect this change.

Guiding principles

Whilst different exam boards adopt different formats, the subject criteria and assessment objectives remain constant, as does the fact that language is language. Oral skills are assessed in AO1 – understand and respond, in speech and writing, to spoken language, and AO2 – understand and respond, in speech and writing, to written language. One can, therefore, extrapolate a general set of principles which can be applied for teaching oral skills.

i   **Building**. Building is the key principle. In order to gain confidence, students should start small and build up, both in terms of lexis and execution.

ii **A mixed skill approach**. It is advisable to adopt a mixed skill approach from the beginning so that speaking is not neglected. This is in keeping with assessment objectives. The target language is the desired medium for the 'A' level classroom.

iii **The interest factor**. This is, in all spheres of teaching, an important principle to adhere to. If teachers are bored by their theme, then pupils cannot fail to be also. Being student friendly in the selection of one's material, involving students in the choice of topics to be studied, and collecting and using material in the target language which is of interest to sixteen to eighteen-year olds often results in their engagement with the subject.

iv **Having opinions**. The fact that students at times have few opinions in their mother tongue makes it necessary for the language teacher to proffer opinions/views that can be either accepted or rejected. The language with which to express these opinions should be taught formally. 'Near fluency' demands more than *A mon avis....*[1] or *Meiner Meinung nach*.

v   **Ownership**. Paradoxically, whilst a teacher may have been instrumental in providing an opinion, it is essential that the student adopts it as her own, if she is to speak with authority and conviction. Students can be involved in the acquisition of their views and vocabulary by such techniques as brainstorming, in English and in the target language, identifying key words, creating their own spider diagrams. Even in the days of child-centred learning and learning by doing, there is a lot to be said for some initial spoon-feeding!

vi **Knowledge**. Students need to have access to relevant facts to support arguments. They must know where to look, how to select and how to present their information.

vii Empowerment. Confidence in their own views and their ability to express them. This can only be gained via the building process, word after word, sentence after sentence.

Assisting in the building process – an attempt to define 'A' level oral methodology

Teachers have a tendency to believe that something miraculous occurs in the hiatus from June to September of the GCSE year. Students are transformed into competent linguists without even opening their vocabulary books. In fact, they may have forgotten or grown rusty over the holidays. The metamorphosis is startling! Experienced teachers – including myself – forget about the endless techniques that they use to engage students at the start of the language learning process and pitch their lessons too high. It is instructive to review all of Programmes of Study Part I, all of that which Marian Carty terms the 'creative rucksack'[2], in order to maintain the level of involvement, spontaneity and fun that one finds in many departments at Key Stage 3. Games work at 'A' level too.

The following are examples of techniques that teachers can use to bring variety to oral work.

- Brainstorming – already mentioned above – is an invaluable technique for stimulating ideas and increasing vocabulary. Translating words in English involves valuable use of dictionaries. It results in a sharing of knowledge.

- Reactions to pictures, first impressions of images are a useful starting point on which to build. Possibly leading to pairwork or groupwork reporting back findings. Overhead transparencies of newspaper or magazine pictures provide up-to-date or unusual starting points.

- Note-taking from listening passages, assistants speaking, the teacher speaking or other students contributing, is a useful activity to expand on a topic.

- Oral or mental remapping of phrases or ideas. Reworking in different directions.

- Being required to adopt a particular point of view on a subject, which is not necessarily one's own.

- Anticipating other people's arguments in a debate.

- Acting as the examiner for general conversation, preparing questions for each other.

- Taking part in debates, discussions and presentations.

- Being required to redraft work orally – to enrich and refine the first attempt.

- Making tapes and videos.

- Being involved in dramatic improvisation.

- Operating in different contexts – using PGCE students/assistants to set up intensive workshops/round tables

Oral skills

Oral skills should be mapped into the course. Whatever the context, it would be helpful to teach students how to:

- express agreement, disagreement and uncertainty;

- offer an opinion;

- use filler phrases

- give an oral presentation supported by notes;

- give an oral presentation without notes;

- improve their register, via reading and listening perhaps;

- analyse images;

- analyse statistics;

- guide discussion in their own direction, onto their own territory;

- counter arguments successfully.

Vocabulary should be provided for this purpose.

General conversation

Different exam formats do not detract from the necessity of students being able to respond to a general question on any unprepared topic. 'A' level linguists at the end of their course must be able to operate in such circumstances. Again, it is essential that discussions of a general nature are not bolt on. Lively, relevant, spontaneous discussion often offers an excellent start to all language lessons. Students bringing in headlines or reporting orally on something they may have heard or on a matter of interest or concern to them is commendable. Such interest in current events often makes for dynamic exchanges. Good use of vocabulary books or designated vocabulary cards for revision of different topics is to be encouraged. Students could aim to produce conversation revision cards with relevant opinions on all of the 'A' level topics outlined by the relevant syllabus.

A case study – *La violence à la télé*

Aim To provide thought provoking materials and approaches to enable students to express themselves in a sophisticated manner on this controversial topic.

In line with the theory outlined above, the following tasks aim to encourage initial formation of ideas, to offer opinions for acceptance or rejection, to then move from the concrete to the abstract and finally to result in the preparation of a presentation. These tasks would of course form part of a mixed skill approach, backed up by listening, reading and writing.

Facts and examples can be garnered from the material offered for their consumption.

Travail oral 1 Faites un remue-méninges sur la violence à la télé. Partagez-vos idées avec celles de votre classe.

(A good way of encouraging students to marshal their thoughts. First impressions are always revealing. What sort of vocabulary will they need to operate in this domain? Where will they find it? Dictionaries, vocab. books, assistants, textbooks. Brainstorming brings the bones of the operation.)

Travail oral 2 Avec lesquelles des opinions ci-dessous êtes-vous d'accord? Faites deux listes.

(Task 2 offers longer utterances for acceptance or rejection. Students may be taken by a phrase or two and decide to add it to their repertoire. At this point, they need to be thinking about their stance.)

	Oui	Non
La banalisation de la violence n'a aucun rapport avec le crime dans la société.		
La radio est un médium qui attire les enfants.		
La télé n'a aucune valeur.		
Des fois les émissions ont une valeur éducative.		
Les questions d'actualité n'ont aucun intéret pour les jeunes.		
On devrait diffuser les films violents plus tard le soir.		
On devrait considérer les effets des jeux vidéo sur les jeunes.		
Les programmes bas de gamme dominent nos écrans.		
La télé encourage la passivité.		
Les jeunes ne sont pas affectés par les images violentes.		
Les familles des téléspectateurs ne se parlent plus.		
Les enfants restent cloués devant la télé.		

Travail oral 3 Regardez cette image. Qu'est-ce que vous voyez? Expliquez la phrase de la mère. Pensez-vous que cette image soit efficace?

(A much more open task encouraging students to express an opinion regarding the influence of television, thus moving from the concrete to the abstract, but providing vocabulary necessary to describe an image and some pointers for expressing opinions.)

Cartoon by Willem, *Libération*, 12/3/98

Des phrases pour décrire une image

Au premier plan   À gauche   On peut discerner

À droite

Sur l'image   Cela donne une impression   Il s'agit de

Des phrases pour exprimer votre opinion

J'estime que   Je pense que   Il me semble que

Travail oral 4 Que pensez-vous de la violence à la télé? Aurait-elle une influence néfaste sur la société? Pensez vous qu'on ait tendance à exagérer l'importance de la télé? La télé, aurait-elle une valeur positive? Préparez une réponse orale à ces questions en vous servant des idées et du vocabulaire ci-dessous.

... pour introduire les phrases

Evidemment	C'est-à-dire que
Il est évident que	Il faut constater que
L'expérience nous montre que	Tout semble indiquer que
Il va de soi que	Il faut réfléchir à
Il va sans dire que	Il faudrait considérer

Les noms ...

les émissions scolaires	les programmes bas de gamme
un moyen d'évasion	la diffusion de certaines images
la course à l'audience	les programmes haut de gamme
le niveau de violence à la télévision	les émissions violentes
la perception de la violence	la censure
les films pornographiques	les téléspectateurs
la banalisation de la violence	le voyeurisme
les documentaires	l'accord parental
une valeur éducative	
le spectacle d'aggression sur le petit écran	

Les adjectifs ...   Les verbes ...

inquiétant	jouer un rôle énorme
perturbant	fausser la perception de la réalité
nuisible	briser les tabous
interdit	influencer
divertissant	exiger

... pour exprimer vos opinions

Moi, personnellement ...	je considère que
	j'estime que
	je trouve que
Pour ma part ...	
Mon opinion, c'est que ...	
D' après moi ...	
Je suis d'accord	Mais non!
Je ne suis pas d'accord	Vous avez tort.
Je ne suis pas du tout de cet avis	

(Further vocabulary to improve the quality of language in this debate could be provided.)

Conclusion

Building up oral skills produces confident well-prepared language learners, who are equipped to take risks and succeed. Encouraging lively debate throughout the course by actively working on oral skills produces linguists who are able to react positively and who are not reliant on pre-learnt material. The goal is to produce candidates who have their own linguistic resources. We as teachers must tap into these and extend them little by little from day one of the 'AS' or 'A' level course.

Appendix 1: Top tips for 'A' level

1 JUSTIFY   HYPOTHESIZE

   COMPARE   TAKE INITIATIVE

   ANALYSE   EXPLORE IDEAS

   EXPLAIN   COMMENT

   CONTRADICT OPINION

2 **Prepare sentences using:**
   i   the subjunctive
   ii 'although ...'
   iii the passive
   iv *si ...*

3 **Ask questions of the examiner**

Appendix 2: Examples of questions

Examples of the types of questions which might be asked in Section (iii) of the oral:

1   What subjects are you studying for 'A' levels?

2   What are your plans for next year?

3   How did you prepare for your university interview?

4   Why do we bother to learn foreign languages when everybody else in the world speaks English?

5   Have you travelled much?

6   What sorts of impressions did you have?

7   How do you fill your free time?

8   Has the changing role of women been to the benefit or detriment of women?

9   Why do people take drugs?

10   How would you help someone who took drugs?

11   Television is a waste of time, isn't it?

12   Does it really influence people?

13   How has science transformed modern day life?

14   Should we all be interested in current affairs?

15   Should we keep the monarchy?

16   Is racism a problem in your school/town etc?

17   What do you and your family do to help with conservation?

18   What makes someone a good friend?

19   How would you change your school/town if you had the chance?

20   What would you do with the money if you won the lottery?

These are randomly selected questions. Usually an examiner will range over 3 or 4 topics in Section (iii) and ask several questions on each. If the candidate's responses indicate difficulty with the topic, the examiner will normally pass on to another area.

References

1   'A' level vocabulary books are an excellent source of opinion expressing vocabulary. *Advanced French Vocabulary, Advanced German Vocabulary, Advanced Spanish Vocabulary*; (Mary Glasgow Publications)

2   Rowles D, Carty M and McLachlan A, *Foreign Language Assistants. A guide to good practice,* Pathfinder 32 (CILT, 1998)

Chapter 3

Developing advanced reading skills

Ann Barnes

'Safety experts say school bus passengers should be belted'

'Stolen painting found by tree'

One of the reasons we read is to enjoy ourselves and to be amused. The headlines above illustrate this, but they also demonstrate how easy it is unintentionally to give the wrong message to readers. Obviously, if our learners can both enjoy reading and read intelligently, then we have succeeded. By enjoying it they will be reading for pleasure and out of genuine curiosity, and by reading intelligently, they will better be able to use what they read in their production of the target language and to read with more precision. Imagine not being able to read, being unable to 'crack the code'. Deciphering these apparently strange communication symbols on a page can actually be very exciting.

As we find ourselves in the age of Information and Communications Technology, reading is becoming even more important: to communicate via e-mail and the Web demands fluent reading ability where skills of skimming, selecting and prioritising are vital. In 'AS'/'A' level foreign language courses, the development of reading skills should be a major priority.

This chapter focuses on the following issues:

- reading: from GCSE to 'AS'/'A' level;
- the need to teach reading skills overtly;
- the 'good' reader versus the 'beginning' reader;
- types of reading activity and types of reading text and the skills required;
- teaching reading strategies and some practical suggestions;
- using the dictionary.

The emphasis of the chapter is on helping your learners to read intelligently, to use the whole of their foreign language learning experience to gain as much as possible from their reading in the target language. This does not imply we should expect the learners to become something approaching applied linguists and to analyse sentences to an extreme degree, but that they should be helped to use their grammatical awareness and other knowledge fully. This might involve adapting, or taking a different slant on, what is already done with your 'AS'/'A' level learners. Some of the examples in the chapter are in German, but can be applied across languages.

Reading: from GCSE to 'AS'/'A' level

Reading is the input or key to a lot of advanced foreign language learning. Without reading widely and above all intelligently, learners' writing, speaking and knowledge of language will not develop as well. One of the main reasons for the perceived 'gap' between GCSE and 'AS'/'A' level is the lack of extended reading ability. Quite a few learners starting out on their 'AS'/'A' level will not have encountered many very long texts and will be anxious about this prospect. This anxiety will be intensified if they are confronted too soon with 'AS'/'A' level standard texts and tasks. At the beginning of an 'AS'/'A' level course it is vital that learners continue to follow a successful model of foreign language learning, where their initial optimism and enthusiasm are maintained through informed, and structured, progress. This is even more apparent where learners have a wide range of foreign language learning experiences pre-16.

Suzanne Graham[1] (1997, p2) describes the most common problems of advanced foreign language learners: extensive reading; writing accurately and at length; using grammar correctly; vocabulary acquisition; listening comprehension; oral discussion work; adopting effective study skills and time management. A structured and thoughtful approach to teaching reading skills can help in the vast majority of these areas. For example, overt attention to exactly **how** vocabulary can be recorded from a reading text can increase confidence. Learners' ability to record target language vocabulary and structures correctly with attention paid to gender, infinitive, prepositions, cases, etc cannot be assumed.

The contrast between reading expected at GCSE and that at 'AS'/'A' level is clear when one considers the following factors:

- length of the reading material;
- complexity of linguistic structures;
- breadth of vocabulary;
- range of topics (more abstract, current affairs, etc);
- the types of task learners are expected to complete from their reading.

Graham[1] (1997, p18 and p33, referring to the work of Cummins) explains that this contrast can be seen in terms of the move from basic interpersonal and communicative skills (BICS) to cognitive/academic language proficiency (CALP) at 'AS'/'A' level. Thus a wider repertoire of skills and abilities is demanded, and this cannot be assumed to be at the disposal of learners when they start the course. Reading skills must be demonstrated, taught, and practised.

The need to teach reading skills overtly

There is a need to teach the reading skills which are so necessary at 'AS'/'A' level. This need can be appreciated by considering some factors which most 'AS'/'A' level teachers will recognise. The following phenomena (among others) can be observed in the work of many foreign language learners at 'AS'/'A' level (learners will display a range of the characteristics and are not only one 'type' or another):

- **Learners who manage to 'read every word' yet understand almost nothing of the text overall.** If they fail to absorb the text as a whole – even if they've 'read' and 'understood' – they do not necessarily retain and comprehend. This means that any chance of responding appropriately to the textual material or producing language based on it is lost.

- **Learners who are 'thrown' by one unfamiliar word in the text.** This gap in their perception of the coherence of the text is felt to be a barrier to understanding any meaning. Where individual words are the cause of learners' anxiety or incomprehension, intelligent use of reference materials as well as contextual clues is required. Discrete vocabulary items should not create barriers to understanding where dictionaries are available, and where learners' grammatical awareness is such that use can be made of them. This factor can lead to learners not even bothering to try to read a text.

- **Learners who make connections with other (target language or other language) words where there are none** (e.g. *Gerät* must be something to do with *raten, pièce* is read as 'piece'). The 'mind map' of the learner is sometimes so crude that only the most basic, superficial connections are made. Annotated reading texts can help here.

- **Learners who do not make connections with other (target language or other language) words when they do exist!** In this case, the 'mind map' is not sufficiently developed even to acknowledge that connections within language(s) occur, and the foreign language is regarded almost as something so alien that a learner has to learn specific meanings for each item and no pattern emerges.

- **Learners who lack awareness of common idioms and structures in the target language which ease comprehension.** These can include such apparently straightforward 'patterns' as the main verb at the end of a subordinate clause in German, or structures in the target language equivalent to phrases such as 'as .... as', 'either .... or'. This can be sheer ignorance of what one might call set phrases that learners definitely need to know.

- **Learners who lack a clear understanding of how features such as layout and punctuation can help when reading.** These will include 'argument' phrases and 'link phrases' which form a framework as well as punctuation 'clues' such as semi-colons or exclamation marks. The target language equivalents of 'firstly, secondly, finally', etc and the many other similar signposts are also important.

• **The gap between some learners' passive grammatical awareness and their ability to use such knowledge when reading.** Learners may be able to cite a grammatical rule and recite irregular verbs, but do not apply this surface knowledge in their reading and understanding of texts.

• **An apparent reluctance by some learners to rely on 'common-sense' when reading target language text.** There is determination on the part of some learners to regard the target language as so 'foreign' that it must be difficult and illogical, so when they believe something means one thing, no amount of contradictory evidence in the text will change their mind.

The 'good' reader versus the 'beginning' reader

It could be argued that the phenomena listed in the previous section stem from the inherent contradiction in advanced level foreign language learning. John Bald[2] (1995), discussing beginning readers of English in a special needs context, presents two pictures, the fluent reader and the beginning reader. In teaching a foreign language at 'AS'/'A' level, I believe learners embody **both** types of reader. Both aspects must be taken into account when setting reading tasks and teaching reading explicitly. Good readers (see Bald[2], 1995) participate in a guessing game (see also Barnes and Powell[3], 1996), which involves intelligent improvisation using any means at the learner's disposal (for example, the use of context, orthography). Advanced level learners of a foreign language are usually at the 'good reader' stage in their own language (although that is not guaranteed) and at the 'beginning' reader stage in the target language with, especially, new vocabulary and structures. This dichotomy can prove very frustrating – learners who in their own language are reading relatively fluently, are having to struggle with individual words in the target language.

Types of reading activity and types of reading text

The types of reading activity and the types of text you use in class and for extended reading tasks are clearly vital. (For a further discussion of these and for a checklist of tasks and texts, see Barnes and Powell[3], 1996.) Ensuring learners are exposed to a wide variety of text types and types of reading activity is crucial to develop the range of reading skills necessary at 'AS'/'A' level. Syllabuses at 'AS'/'A' level include reference to a wide range of textual material, and examination papers and course books cover many different types of task, from true/false to searching comprehension questions. To ascertain the current situation for your specific learners, you could ask yourself the following questions:

• Have you got a good 'spread' of **text** types or does most of your material originate from the coursebook or a narrow range of newspapers or magazines? Are a few text types predominating, thus not presenting learners with as wide a range of language as you could?

- Have you got a good 'spread' of **activity** types or do you tend to stick to 'tried and tested' tasks which you know 'work'?

- Are you moving from **recognition** activities to **interpretation** activities too quickly (i.e. are you expecting learners to react to the content of the text before they have had the opportunity to come to grips with the language)? There may be a case for adopting some more text manipulation type activities.

- Do your activities tend to be predominantly too easy or too challenging for much of the time?

- How do you incorporate **reading training** in to the 'AS'/'A' level course – implicitly, explicitly, in an ad hoc manner, not at all?

- How do you and your learners use (and practise the use of) dictionaries in and outside the lessons?

There are many varied **purposes** and **outcomes** to reading activities expected during an 'A'/'AS' level course and in the examinations. From a brief look at one examination paper – which included such tasks as gap fill, a true/false exercise on a fairly long general text, multiple choice requiring grammatical understanding, summary of a written text, a persuasive letter using authentic information in the target language – it is apparent that the advanced level foreign language learner must be able to adapt reading strategies to many purposes, even within the context of one examination paper. Some tasks require very different skills to others. It is important to remember the aims of the course and the syllabus here, and actively to encourage development of the appropriate strategies. If you consider exactly which reading skills learners require to be able to complete the tasks at 'AS'/'A' level, it is clear that they are very demanding. They would be advanced in the learners' native language. Learners are not going to have to do all of these all at once, of course, but introducing and practising a range of reading skills and strategies is necessary.

Teaching reading strategies

Learners need to begin to understand the reading process and the value of strategies. At this point it is crucial to find out what is happening with your learners with regard to learning strategies and difficulties they have. You could ask them to tick which sections from a list of commonly experienced difficulties apply to them (see Graham[1], 1997, Appendix B1). The two activities below have been used with both teachers and 'AS'/'A' level learners to illustrate what is happening when we read, and to emphasise the importance of looking for detail when reading.

Present the group with the following text exactly as it appears below on the overhead projector for a second or two (no more!).

Mary had a
a little lamb.

Ask them what it said. Most of the group is likely to have not read it **exactly**, i.e. they will not have noticed the repeated 'a'. Certain items were expected, the phrase was familiar, and therefore the actual, detailed, content was skipped over.

This same process happens frequently when learners read texts in the target language – they see what they think they should see; whether that is a word that resembles a word in English, or the singular of the noun when it is actually the plural. This is clearly not because the language is as familiar to them as the item above is in English, but because the 'guessing game' is working without the control of detailed observation. The conflict between the fluent reader, who picks up clues and interprets them into a whole, and the beginning reader, who needs to take account of all relevant detail which carries such vital information, is apparent.

The second activity, which I first saw used by Tony Wright[4] (1997), demonstrates this point in a slightly different way. The following text, apparently graffiti seen on a train, scrawled on the seat behind a passenger, is displayed on the OHP to the class. Ask them if they are all aware of the meaning of what they see:

MAN UTD.

Then, when the passenger stood up, the whole text (below) is revealed, thus indicating the need to see and understand **all** 'information' provided when reading to get the full picture:

WOMAN UTD.

Learners need to appreciate the importance of looking at all relevant detail. The analogy with the foreign language could be appreciating the amount of important information such as gender and plural conveyed in adjective endings, for example.

Graham[1] (1997, p52) suggests listeners and readers must be both good interpreters (top down) and good decoders of text (bottom up). Top down suggests making predictions about a text's meaning based on prior experience or knowledge, but also checking text for confirmation or refutation of these predictions. Reading intelligently in this context means checking 'guesses' as one reads further. Bottom up suggests gleaning information from details in words (tenses, singular/plural, etc) and using this information to establish a whole.

Helping learners to read intelligently implies discussing and teaching reading skills and associated strategies explicitly. What sort of strategies can you teach your learners and how? What do you already do? Do you teach them overtly, as they come up, or not very obviously at all? It is important to ensure that the learners see the relevance and benefits of strategies, and do not get the impression that they are yet another thing to worry about. As Graham[1] (1997) emphasises, knowing about learning strategies is not the same as choosing a strategy appropriately. Possessing a list of reading strategies is clearly no guarantee of using any of them, much as a list of vocabulary filed away carefully is no proof that the words have been learnt. Practice and demonstration of the strategies are essential.

A major issue is whether to use the target language for such explicit strategy teaching. I believe that the use of English to discuss strategies is probably beneficial. Where possible, some of this discussion can be conducted in the target language, but the cognitive processes involved are most likely to be clearer if English is the medium of discussion. Graham[1] (1997) used 'thinkaloud' interviews to try to discover strategies used by 'AS'/'A' level learners, for example, when they are grappling with a piece of written target language. Whole group discussion on similar lines can be of benefit, particularly when thinking about an approach to a written text. An overhead transparency of a reading text and/or task can be presented to the group using a variety of techniques. This can help with reading orientation, rubrics, etc.[6]

Some practical suggestions

The following suggestions are possible ways of introducing some reading skills and strategies to your groups. The list could be presented initially with just the key words (see Appendix 1, p35) and, through reference to real target language material, the strategies involved can be highlighted, exemplified and practised.

A target language checklist of helpful words and expressions can also help beginning readers to discover textual frameworks and to orientate themselves. Certain phrases and words will leap to mind that could slot into these categories when reading target language texts. These can then be highlighted to learners and subsequently used in their own target language production – after all, reading provides models and structures for their own writing and foreign language use.

Grammar constitutes a major discussion point. How do you deal with grammar in the first year of 'AS'/'A' level? However it is done, you need to consider what use learners make of it and how to help them make the link between grammar lessons and language development e.g. understand that more accurate grammatical knowledge will help considerably with reading.

Specific reading training activities

The importance of **context** can be illustrated as follows. Show an English text such as the one below, with key words covered up. This is easy to do and can help build learners' confidence. Then do the same with a target language version. (In both examples, the words to cover up are in italics.)

'Bruce vows: I'll clear my *name.*'

'We will tell you where to play, how to play, and where to *claim* your prizes.'

'Of our last 34 Premiership games, we have won 8, drawn 9 and *lost* 17.'

'A robber got 8 years jail yesterday for carrying out raids armed with a *water pistol, rolled up newspapers* and a *sawn-off tennis racquet.*'

'Zwei *Sprengsätze* detonierten in der irakischen Hauptstadt.'

'*Ungeachtet* weltweiter Kritik halten die USA an ihrer Entscheidung fest.'

Apart from use of context, other hints can involve **dissecting target language words** (i.e. working out roots and relationships) and identifying **key words**. Sometimes, when a text is particularly challenging, it might be a good idea to ignore the really difficult words or structures at first and try to get an **overall picture** of the text. Build the sense of the text up gradually and try to identify the key words which you can then look up.

Learners also need practice in **reading for detail and getting all the information.** It is easy to miss some little words that they actually know very well when they are in a hurry to finish something. Such words as *'ziemlich'* (quite), *'sehr'* (very), *'vollkommen'* (completely) add a lot of meaning to the words they accompany. Some words, like *'kaum'* (scarcely), if ignored, can significantly change the meaning of a sentence and, therefore, the text.

One way of increasing learners' reading ability in the target language is, clearly, as with any skill, to **practise** it more! For those learners who do not perhaps read very much in their own language, this is clearly even more important. For example, learners can be encouraged to get hold of some target language magazines and just read the bits they find interesting. With extra reading such as this, they should not feel they have to read every word of every article – would they (or you for that matter) do so in English? When they do find something they want to read, however, they can be encouraged to set themselves a small target – perhaps five new words or phrases from one article. They should then note down what they find and learn them – and the best way to do this is to use them!

Newspaper searches can help with **skimming** and **scanning.** In pairs or groups initially learners have a newspaper and a list of 'categories' to find, ranging from an article about violence, education, an election, or leisure, to a problem page or film review. The category list is the same for each pair or group, but they have different newspapers. Learners then scan the newspapers to find an example for each category, cut each one out, mount them and label as appropriate in the target language. This activity could be carried out in English first to demonstrate the kinds of skills being used. An extension of this involves learners then either identifying and defining key vocabulary and structures from each short article, or creating, for example, true/false statements to accompany the article for other pairs or groups to complete.

A variation involves learners being given articles cut from a newspaper, which have been detached from their headlines. They receive the headlines too and must match them up as appropriate, possibly against the clock. This is good practice for quick, skim type reading, where key words and phrases are important. Again, this could be done briefly using English articles initially to help identify some of the reading processes and skills used. Other practical ideas for developing reading skills in and outside of contact time can be found in Barnes and Powell[3], (1996).

Using the dictionary

Many good books have been published on this topic[5], so I shall merely indicate some of the issues. Using the dictionary can be extremely helpful in the development of reading skills, and successful language learners would see a dictionary as a vital tool for both decoding (comprehending) the target language and encoding (producing) the target language. As many of the publications on dictionary skills make clear, the use of the dictionary must be practised and not simply assumed as a skill which learners will already possess. Teachers of 'AS'/'A' level foreign languages can help learners by highlighting:

• what learners should do before they use a dictionary;
• and how to use a dictionary to its best advantage.

Advice to learners could look similar to that contained in Appendix 2 (p36). As learners work their way up through KS3 and 4, the use of the dictionary should in theory become more familiar to them. Most of the actual techniques for using a dictionary do not change extensively when the language studied is at a more advanced level as far as the mechanics are concerned.

Conclusion – helping learners to read intelligently

Reading intelligently and developing appropriate skills and strategies is vital when studying a foreign language effectively. Improved reading ability can inform the whole of the foreign language learning experience for the learner and form a solid basis for future study. For example, reading intelligently should help learners choose the correct word for the purpose of their writing. The more they read and the more they practise reading strategies, the more they will know when to use particular words or structures and when not to. If the language **input** isn't processed properly by the learner, the **output** will not be as successful.

References

1   Graham S, *Effective language learning* (Clevedon: Multilingual Matters, 1997)

2   Bald J, 'A case of the wrong identity' in *TES* p40 (14 April 1995)

3   Barnes A and B Powell, *Concepts 8: Developing advanced reading skills* (MGP/ Stanley Thornes, 1996)

4   Wright T, 'Doing language awareness in teacher education', paper presented at the 1997 IALS symposium, *Language in language teacher education – new directions*? (University of Edinburgh, 14 November 1997)

5   See, for example, Berwick G and P Horsfall, *Making effective use of the dictionary*, Pathfinder 28 (CILT, 1996)

6   Some ideas for using the OHP for whole class strategy discussion are to be found in Barnes A and G Pomfrett, 'Assessment in German at KS3: How can it be consistent, fair and appropriate?', in *German Teaching,* 17: 2–6 (March 1998) and Barnes A and S Graham, *Concepts 11: Target Language Testing* (MGP/Stanley Thornes, 1998)

Appendix 1: Introducing reading skills and strategies: checklist

Headlines or title: can give lots of clues.

Sub-titles: within an article can help provide a framework of the content of the article.

Scanning: the text, getting the gist of it, finding your way around it. Note any difficult items that suddenly come to you while you're reading – they've got a tendency to fall out of your brain for some reason when you go back to them if you don't make a note straightaway!

Type: of text. Journalistic? Advertising? Literature? Is there obviously dialogue in the text?

Predict: the sort of language the text will contain.

Illustrations: if there are any, look at these carefully. They may not, however, give you any clues at all, and they may even mislead you!

Captions: if there are any, what sort of language may appear in the text when thinking about the images.

Statistics/ diagrams: they may tell you what sort of arguments the text is likely to contain.

Task:	what are you expected to complete? Work out exactly what you need to do to tackle it efficiently. Decide how you're going to use the text to complete the task.
Logic/ common sense:	Occasionally, texts will contain contradictory information. Mostly, however, they will follow a logical argument and make sense. Therefore whatever you write in response has also to be logical and consistent! Re-read what you have written for different parts of the task – does what you write rule out something else you have written?

Appendix 2: Advice to learners

Before you use a dictionary

Whatever you do, try to get into the habit of trying to work the meaning out before you look the word up or ask the teacher. Split the words up and try to work out where they come from. What can you get from the context of the sentence? How can you use logic to help you?

Using the dictionary

The main thing to remember when using a dictionary is not to use it too much! Many other strategies which you will practise in class will help you understand and use the target language – the dictionary will not solve all your problems. It could even create problems for you if you don't use it properly. For example, you could use the wrong word and end up saying something completely nonsensical. One way of avoiding this, if you are using a bilingual dictionary, is to look the word up in the other half of the dictionary to check its meaning. You have to use a dictionary intelligently and like a useful tool – it cannot learn and produce the target language for you.

When thinking about using the dictionary, ask yourself:

• do I really need to look up or know every word I don't know straightaway?

Try this with a text which you are finding problematic:

• underline all the words/phrases that you don't understand. Then choose the three you think you definitely will need to look up to get the meaning sorted out.

Practise identifying these key words in the target language you read and then looking them up and making sure you look them up efficiently and correctly.

Chapter 4

Discovering literature through the target language – a first reading of Maupassant's *Boule de suif*

Sheila Barbour

Anyone who has learned a foreign language well enough to read its literature in the original knows the anguish of struggling through their first text. With a dictionary at their side, looking up every third word, struggling to identify a verb form, they are pleased to have read two pages in an hour! Teachers appreciate that this may be the experience which finally turns their students off and they try to find ways of easing them into the text. When I was an 'A' level student preparing to read Maupassant's *Quinze contes*, our teacher opted against tackling the text at all and instead started with dictated notes which began: 'Short story writing is a difficult art......' Even as an uncritical sixteen-year old I thought that something was amiss here. Many more imaginative teaching approaches have been tried and coincidentally I came across one while browsing through Mary Glasgow's *Thématique 9* just before giving the talk on which this paper is based. In *Thématique 9* the aim is to link a number of extracts from French literature to the theme of war. *Boule de Suif* is one of the texts used, but the assumption is that students will already have read the text. But how? How do they set about such a task? These are the difficulties I hope to tackle. What strategies can we adopt to make a 19th century story, full of military and other abstruse vocabulary and dated political allusions, accessible, palatable or even enjoyable? The first reading of a literary text takes a long time. Time is limited. We cannot allow our students to sit passively lesson after lesson while we plough through the text. How can they be actively involved in the process and be using the target language themselves during those lessons?

Whenever we begin a book, we begin in ignorance. We don't know what is going to happen, we don't know anything about the characters. Skilful writers will make us want to know. Our students will understand this, but I suggest making them articulate this knowledge before we start reading. In the exercise below students are presented with very different opening lines from four novels in the target language, here French. They are asked to compare the ways in which the authors have tried to engage the readers' interest and whether they have succeeded. Would they continue reading these novels? If yes why, or why not? This initiates discussion in the target language of what goes through our minds when we read the first pages of a novel:

__Qu'est-ce qu'un auteur doit faire dans les premières pages d'un roman?__

Comparez ces quatres débuts de roman. Quelles méthodes les auteurs emploient-ils pour arriver à leur but?

Est-ce que vous continueriez de lire ces romans? Pourquoi? Pourquoi pas?

1 'Aujourd'hui maman est morte. Ou peut-être hier. Je ne sais pas.'

(Albert Camus, *L'Etranger*)[1]

2 '*Chambre de la fin*
Penang, Malaisie. 17 juin 1982

A haute et intelligible voix, sans haine ni passion, le juge Lee se met à lire:

Cette cour ordonne que vous, Béatrice Saubin, soyez conduite de cette enceinte jusqu'à une prison, puis de là vers un lieu d'exécution où vous subirez la mort par pendaison.

La salle d'audience est toujours là. C'est moi qui ai disparu.
Tout est figé. Même la foule.
Je suis glacée.
Pourquoi la mort?'

(Béatrice Saubin, *L'Epreuve*)[2]

3 'La seule façon de résumer la situation au moment où je me retrouve dans la cour, tout seul et les mains vides, le passé mort et l'avenir pas encore né, c'est: ils me font tous chier.'

(Christiane Rochefort, *Printemps au Parking*)[3]

4 'L'avocat ouvrit la porte. Thérèse Desqueyroux, dans ce couloir dérobé du palais de justice, sentit sur sa face la brume et profondément l'aspira. Elle avait peur d'être attendue, hésitait à sortir.'

(François Mauriac, *Thérèse Desqueroux*)[4]

My experience is that students talk a lot during this activity and I hope it helps them to accept that ignorance is normal and inevitable when one starts out on a book, and that their ignorance of the French text they are about to read will not be totally due to the fact that the book is in French. (Fuller details of students' responses to this activity can be found in my book *Discovering literature through the target language,* to be published by CILT.)

I have chosen Maupassant's *Boule de Suif* to illustrate some of the methods I suggest for a first reading of the text which will enable students to use the target language to the maximum. The key role of the teacher is to select sections of the text for close study and to guide the students to those passages that are most helpful for their initial understanding. Attempts to encompass everything at first reading would be disastrous. The activities I propose have three aims:

* to enable the students to find their way into the text;

* to enable the teacher to check their comprehension;

* to enable the students to examine language closely and to draw their own conclusions based on **evidence**.

Finding a way into the text

The first activity is based on Section A of the chosen text.

Section A

> Pendant plusiers jours de suite des lambeaux d'armeé en déroute avaient traversé la ville. Ce n'était point de la troupe, mais des hordes débandées. Les hommes avaient la barbe longue et sale, des uniformes en guenilles, et ils avançaient d'une allure molle, sans drapeau, sans régiment. Tous semblaient accablés, éreintés, incapables d'une pensée ou d'une résolution, marchant seulement par habitude, et tombant de fatigue sitôt qu'ils s'arrêtaient. On voyait surtout des mobilisés, gens pacifiques, rentiers tranquilles, pliant sous le poids de fusil; des petits moblots alertes, faciles à l'épouvante et prompts à l'enthousiasme, prêts à l'attaque comme à la fuite; puis, au milieu d'eux, quelques culottes rouge, débris d'une division moulue dans une grande bataille; des artilleurs sombres alignés avec ces fantassins divers; et, parfois, le casque brillant d'un dragon au pied pesant qui suivait avec peine la marche plus légère des lignards.
>
> Des légions de francs-tireurs aux appellations héroïques: 'Les Vengeurs de la Défaite – Les Citoyens de las Tombe – les Partageurs de la Mort' – passaient à leur tour, avec des airs de bandits.
>
> Leurs chefs, anciens commerçants en draps ou en graines, ex-marchands de suif ou de savon, guerriers de circonstance, nommés officiers pour leurs écus ou la longueur de leurs moustaches, couverts d'armes, de flanelle et de galons, parlaient d'une voix retentissante, discutaient plans de campagne, et prétendaient soutenir seuls la France agonisante sur leurs épaules de fanfarons; mais ils redoutaient parfois leurs propres soldats, gens de sac et de corde, souvent braves à outrance, pillards et débauchés.
>
> Les Prussians allaient entrer dans Rouen, disait-on.

It invites students to explore the text for clues, in the first place to answer the broad question of what is going on, *De quoi s'agit-il*?

No dictionaries to be used here because I want my students to see **how much they can discover from language they already know**. A typical outcome is given in (i) below.

i   **De quoi s'agit-il dans le premier paragraphe? Cherchez les indications.**

They will recognise certain words, such as *armée, troupe, uniformes, régiment, attaque, une grande bataille* and possibly *fusil* and *mobilisés,* and thus will be able to reach a conclusion:

Donc: **il s'agit d'une armée, de la guerre.**

The next stage, still based on section A, asks the students to go a stage further using a monolingual dictionary to study several phrases and draw conclusions.

ii   **Considérez les phrases suivantes. Quelle conclusion en tirez-vous?**

'des **lambeaux** d'armée en **déroute**'
'des **hordes débandés**'
'des uniformes en **guenilles**'
'des mobilisés ......**pliant sous le poids du fusil**'
'prêts à l'attaque comme à **la fuite**'
'**débris** d'une division **moulue dans une grande bataille**'

Understanding of the words in heavy type will lead to a conclusion:

Donc: **il s'agit d'une armée vaincue.**

Two simple questions …

iii   **Laquelle? Vaincue par qui?**

… call for answers to establish that the setting is the Franco-Prussian war.

Now the teacher, acting as guide and knowing that Maupassant wanted to emphasise the utter defeat of the French army, can ask the students to use their monolingual dictionary to explore a little further his choice of words to convey this rout.

iv   **Trouvez d'autres phrases/mots dans le premier paragraphe qui suggèrent**

La défaite	**La fatigue**
sans drapeau	la barbe longue et sale
sans régiment	accablés
la fuite	éreintés
des artilleurs sombres	incapables d'une pensée
alignés avec des fantassins	dragon au pied pesant
divers	pliant sous le poids du fusil
	marchant seulement par habitude
	tombant de fatigue

Some of this language will be easily accessible, e.g. *tombant de fatigue, sans régiment,* and this will hopefully be a boost to confidence; other items, requiring dictionary work, will yield new words to add to active vocabulary, e.g. *accablés, la fuite, le poids du fusil.*

Finally, to foster awareness of Maupassant's irony, I suggest the following:

v **Lesquels des mots sur la liste ci-dessous décrivent le mieux les chefs de l'armée :**

   orgeuilleux vantards prétentieux lâches patriotiques ridicules courageux

The range of possible answers provides a mix of more and less accessible items.

So far my experience has been that someone in the class will suggest an appropriate answer to my last question:

vi **Le ton de Maupassant est donc ...?**

   ironique, moqueur

The key to this first activity, then, is a blend of the students' existing knowledge with guided use of their monolingual dictionary to explore the unknown. The text gradually becomes accessible through their own active involvement, using the target language and adding judiciously to their own vocabulary.

Checking comprehension

Here I will briefly suggest some very familiar and well-tried exercises. It is important not to forget methodical exercises of this kind amongst the others which might seem more exciting and creative. I suggest gap-fill summaries of short sections to be done in class at frequent intervals and without dictionaries. Multiple choice exercises are useful and, as oral activities, individuals may be asked to summarise a brief section from memory or the teacher may provide an oral summary with deliberate mistakes to be spotted and instantly corrected by the class. It is important to collect written work to check each individual's grasp of the story – we will all be able to cite instances of staggering misunderstandings!

Close examination of language, leading to conclusions based on evidence

The social microcosm which Maupassant creates in the coach carrying the travellers to Dieppe needs to be understood in detail. To appreciate how he creates this microcosm, we need to study the language used in Section B of the extract.

Section B

Tout au fond, aux meilleures places, sommeillaient, en face l'un de l'autre, M. et Mme Loiseau, des marchands de vin en gros de la rue Grand-Pont.

Ancien commis d'un patron ruiné dans les affaires, Loiseau avait acheté le fonds et fait fortune. Il vendait à tres bon marché de très mauvais vin aux petits débitants des campagnes et passait parmi ses connaissances et ses amis pour un fripon madré, un vrai Normand plein de ruses et de jovialité.

Sa réputation de filou était si bien établie, qu'un soir, à la préfecture, M. Tournel, auteur de fables et de chansons, esprit mordant et fin, une gloire locale, avait proposé aux dames qu'il voyait un peu somnolentes de faire une partie de 'Loiseau vole'; le mot lui-même vola à travers les salons du préfet, puis, gagnant ceux de la ville, avait fait rire pendant un mois toutes les mâchoires de la province.

Loiseau était en outre célèbre par ses farces de toute nature, ses plaisanteries bonnes ou mauvaises; et personne ne pouvait parler de lui sans ajouter immédiatement: 'Il est impayable, ce Loiseau.'

De taille exiguë, il présentait un ventre en ballon surmonté d'une face rougeaude entre deux favoris grisonnants.

Sa femme, grande, forte, résolue, avec la voix haute et la décision rapide, était l'ordre et l'arithmétique de la maison de commerce, qu'il animait par son activité joyeuse.

A côté d'eux se tenait, plus digne, appartenant à une caste supérieure, M. Carré-Lamadon, homme considérable, posé dans les coton, propriétaire de trois filatures, officier de la Légion d'honneur et membre du Conseil général. Il était resté tout le temps de l'Empire chef de l'opposition bienveillante, uniquement pour se faire payer plus cher son ralliement à la cause qu'il combattait avec des armes courtoises, selon sa propre expression. Mme Carré-Lamadon, beaucoup plus jeune que son mari, demeurait la consolation des officiers de bonne famille envoyés à Rouen en garnison.

Elle faisait vis-à-vis à son époux, toute petite, toute mignonne, toute jolie, pelotonnée dans ses fourrures, et regardait d'un œil navré l'intérieur lamentable de la voiture.

Ses voisins, le comte et la comtesse Hubert de Bréville, portaient un des noms les plus anciens et les plus nobles de Normandie. Le comte, vieux gentilhomme de grande tournure, s'efforçait d'accentuer, par les artifices de sa toilette, sa ressemblance naturelle avec le roy Henri IV, qui, suivant une légende glorieuse pour la famille, avait rendu grosse une dame de Bréville, dont le mari, pour ce fait, étiat devenu comte et gouverneur de province.

Collègue de M. Carré-Lamadon au Conseil général, le comte Hubert représentait le parti orléaniste dans le département. L'histoire de son mariage avec la fille d'un petit armateur de Nantes était toujours demeurée mystérieuse. Mais, comme la comtesse avait grand air, recevait mieux que personne, passait même pour avoir été aimée par un des fils de Louis-Philippe, toute la noblesse lui faisait fête, et son salon demeurait le premier du pays, le seul où se conservât la vieille galanterie, et dont l'entrée fût difficile.

La fortune des Bréville, toute en biens-fonds, atteignait, disait-on, cinq cent mille livres de revenu.

Ces six personnes formaient le fond de la voiture, le côté de la société rentée, sereine et forte, des honnêtes gens autorisés qui ont de la Religion et des Principes.

I ask my students to create a table headed …

Nom	Physique	Classe sociale/Profession	Caractère

… and to comb the text for details about each character. This is a major task to be shared among the class and done at home. Back in class results can be pooled and memorable phrases brought out for the first time: Madame Loiseau, *l'ordre et l'arithmétique de la maison*; Monsieur Carré-Lamadon, belonging to *une caste supérieure*; Madame Carré-Lamadon, *la consolation des officiers de bonne famille*; Monsieur Loiseau, *Loiseau vole.* Under the teacher's guidance the class can now use their dictionaries to discover the connotations of *caste* – '*groupe social fermé … d'abord en Inde*', and discuss why Maupassant chose this particular word. Similarly *consolation – consoler* – '*soulager quelqu'un dans son chagrin*'. (*Quel genre de soulagement Mme Carré-Lamadon offre-t-elle?*) It is important to gather together students' ideas on the board as we go along, but then afterwards to draw together their discoveries and pinpoint the most significant. I suggest here OHT's using different colours for different columns. The visual impression will underline what has been discovered – in which column is there the greatest amount of detail, where is there almost none? It can be seen that *Classe sociale/profession* is the fullest column and for some characters there is no physical detail given at all. Students may therefore infer from this evidence that social class is important in this story.

Close study of the paragraph labelled Section C reveals a great deal.

Section C

> La femme, une de celles appelées galantes, était célèbre par son embonpoint précoce qui lui avait valu le surnom de Boule de Suif. Petite, ronde de partout, grasse à lard, avec des doigts bouffis, étranglés aux phalanges, pareils à des chapelets de courtes saucisses, avec une peau luisante et tendue, une gorge énorme qui saillait sous sa robe, elle restait cependant appétissante et courue, tant sa fraîcheur faisait plaisir à voir. Sa figure était une pomme rouge, un bouton de pivoine prêt à fleurir, et là-dedans s'ouvraient, en haut, deux yeux noirs magnifiques, ombragés de grands cils épais qui mettaient une ombre dedans; en bas, une bouche charmante, étroite, humide pour le baiser, meublée de quenottes luisantes et microscopiques.
>
> Elle était de plus, disait-on, pleine de qualités inappréciables.

First of all the amount of physical detail in the description of *Boule de Suif* is in sharp contrast to the other characters. We might speculate why, but first to help students to discover this for themselves I ask them:

Dans la description de *Boule de Suif* quelles comparaisons voyez-vous? Quelles allusions Maupassant fait-il?

Although much of the vocabulary needs looking up, there are immediate items which stand out – *une pomme rouge, courtes saucisses*. This activity takes effort and needs close guidance, but eventually associations with fat, meal, nature and appetising food emerge. The subtle associations of these images are worth pursuing and again I suggest colour coding the results. As well as raising awareness of the sophistication of language at this level, this activity extends everyday vocabulary and, very importantly, draws attention to the deficiencies of translation: *des chapelets de courtes saucisses* / strings of short sausages completely loses the allusion to the rosary and thus the association with the piety and *La Religion* of the nuns and the other 'respectable' members of the group. A strong argument, I believe, for approaching texts directly in the target language rather than having early recourse to translation or the intermediary of editors' notes.

Here is a suggested summary of the work on Section C is given on the following page:

A summary of the work I suggest on Section C is produced in part below. This provides an opportunity for detailed dictionary work and I suggest presenting the results in a way that is visually striking. Associations with fat, meat, nature and appetising food may be colour coded on an OHT.

Examples:

- Looking up *embonpoint* will lead to the definition *un corps un peu gras* and to *corpulence.* We might colour code *gras* in red and then do the same with other words associated with the idea of fat, e.g. *grasse, doigts bouffis, une gorge énorme.*

- Investigation of *précoce* leads us to *mûr avant son temps,* with associations with *fruits* and *fleurs*. Colour coding these words, with their associations with nature, in green helps us to see the connections more clearly. *Un bouton de pivoine prêt à fleurir* would also be in green.

- One further example of significant associations to be grouped together would be words evoking appetising food – *des chapelets de courtes saucisses, une pomme rouge* and the word *appétissante* itself. The definition of this last word *qu'on a envie de manger* is followed by *appétits sexuels,* a theme central to the story.

The students are thus discovering the richness of associations themselves through guided dictionary work, and seeing the results presented visually in this way may enhance their appreciation of Maupassant's skill with the French language.

Detailed examination of this section may heighten the student reader's awareness of images used elsewhere: the stark contrast with *la dure carcasse* of Mme Loiseau and the range of associations, wholesome and otherwise, raised by *appétissante* and *appétit* which may be appreciated near the end of the story in the voyeurism of the respectable ladies *'tripotant de l'amour avec la sensualité d'un cuisinier gourmand qui prépare le souper d'un autre.'*

La description de Boule de Suif

Son embonpoint précoce

embonpoint
    ⤷ un corps un peu gras
        ⤷'bien en chair → corpulence'

précoce
    ⤷ qui est mûr avant le temps normal
      ⤷ fruit, graine

grasse à lard
    ⤷ la graisse du porc
des chapelets de courtes saucisses
    ⤷ objet de dévotion ... les prières
             ⤷ les bonnes sœurs,
               la Religion

doigts bouffis
    ⤷ gonflés
une gorge énorme qui saillait
appétissante
    ⤷ qu'on a envie de manger
    ⤷ l'appétit: 'le désir de manger'
        'désir pressant'
        'appétits sexuels'
           ⤷ *plaisir à voir*

une pomme rouge
    ⤷ *peau luisante et tendue*

sa fraîcheur
    ⤷ *un bouton de pivoine prêt à fleurir*

deux yeux magnifiques ombragés de grands cils
         ⤷ 'ombrager → feuillages ... arbres
           qui ombragent une allée'
pleine de qualités
    ⤷ un produit de qualité

Section D

> Les femmes se serrèrent, le ton de la voix fut baissé, et la discussion devint générale, chacun donnant son avis. C'était fort convenable du reste. Ces dames surtout trouvaient des delicatesses de tournures, des subtilités d'expression charmantes, pour dire les choses les plus scabreuses. Un étranger n'aurait rien compris tant les précautions du langage étaient observées. Mais la légère tranche de pudeur dont est bardée toute femme du monde ne recouvrant que la surface, elles s'épanouissaient dans cette aventure polissonne, s'amusaient follement au fond, se sentant dans leur élément, tripotant de l'amour avec la sensualité d'un cuisinier gourmand qui prépare le souper d'un autre.

Conclusion

What I have suggested here are strategies for involving students actively in the first reading of the text. Pace is important and between the sections I have singled out for close study I am prepared to go fast, translating as necessary and maintaining the pace of the narrative. *Boule de Suif* is quite short; longer works require adaptation of this approach, but the principle of active involvement and discovery remains. Subsequent readings allow us to elaborate points further and allow scope for individual students to prepare commentaries on sections we have initially skipped over. Those wishing to prepare fuller studies of the work may now read other stories and/or works of criticism (in French or English.) My concern here has been with devising ways of allowing everyone access to the text through their own active use of French.

References

1   Camus A, *L'Etranger.* Collection Folio; © Editions Gallimard, Paris, 1942

2   Saubin B, *L'Epreuve.* Editions Robert Laffont, Paris, 1991

3   Rochefort C, *Printemps au Parking.* Editions Bernard Grasset, Paris, 1969

4   Mauriac F, *Thérèse Desqueroux.* Editions Bernard Grasset, Paris, 1927; Livre de Poche 1967

Chapter 5

Teaching history and culture through the modern foreign language

Hilary Barker

In this chapter I shall be discussing how to build up an integrated language dossier for able 'A' level students by introducing them to a particular period of twentieth century French history. The aim is not only to enhance language skills and awareness, but also to teach them how to go about personal research and to foster their own curiosity concerning the background to contemporary issues in the target language country.

Rationale

One of the aims made explicit in the post-Dearing overhaul of 'A' level language syllabuses is that students should study in depth **aspects of the society and culture** of the countries whose language is being studied. They are also required to use the target language 'to analyse, hypothesise, evaluate, argue a case, justify, persuade, rebut, develop arguments and present viewpoints, in speech and in writing'. In the last year, with the help of a motivated group of lower sixth formers, I have started to implement these objectives by compiling a dossier entitled *La France pendant la Deuxième Guerre Mondiale: Collaboration et Résistance*. The choice of topic presented itself quite naturally from the curiosity of pupils to explore such issues as guilt, responsibility, historical fact, cultural determinism and political expediency, an interest which is, in my experience, perennial because of the momentous nature of what took place in Europe between 1939 and 1945. Pupils, contrary to what might be assumed of them, find these issues precisely of relevance to themselves and what is happening in the 1990s: my students, for example, understood very quickly how such study was pertinent to the Papon trial and the rise of the far-right.

Structure

I did, nevertheless, depart from an assumption of almost total ignorance of the period. In order to whet students' appetite, I began with a clip from Louis Malle's well-known study of collaboration and heroism *Au Revoir Les Enfants*. The scene chosen was that in which Jean Bonnet, hiding the fact of his Jewishness, witnesses anti-Semitic aggression by the French militia in a restaurant reserved for Aryans; the militia are sent packing by German officers trying to eat their meal in peace. It was presented to the class without prior explanation other than to give the period. Immediately questions are raised: the ambiguities of occupation; the role of collaborators; the common decency of the enemy; the implications of being an outsider; the power of fear. Students'; interest is invariably aroused. The usual image that 6th formers have, if they have one at all, is that France resisted Nazi occupation valiantly. If they know of the Resistance, they know little of the internecine warfare between '*groupes francs*', *Maquis*, communist agitators and, later, untrained resistants and turncoats, nor of the rivalry between those groups that stayed put and de Gaulle who was sometimes perceived as having taken the easy option in fleeing to England. Vichy, Pétain, French anti-Semitism, the extent of elimination of French Jews and the role of the militia are hardly ever known at all.

Pupils are then asked to consider the following series of questions and discussion points.

AU REVOIR LES ENFANTS

Scène du restaurant

Questions à discuter

1. Quelle est l'atmosphère avant l'arrivée de la milice?

2. Imaginez les pensées de Jean Bonnet dans le restaurant face aux questions de son hôtesse. Comment est-ce que vous décririez son attitude à elle?

3. Considérez la façon don't se comportent les gens de la milice avec le vieux monsieur avant et après qu'il montre ses papiers. Qu'est-ce que cela suggère?

4. En quoi le patron du restaurant diffère-t-il de la milice? Comment les autres clients réagissent-ils et pourquoi?

5. La milice travaille à coté de et en quelque sorte sous l'égide des occupants nazis. Comment est-ce que vous décririez la conduite des officiers allemands? Vous la trouvez surprenante ou non? Pourquoi? Qu'est-ce que le cinéaste Louis Malle essaie de faire?

6. Quels seraient les adjectifs que vous utiliseriez pour décrire cette scène? Qu'est-ce vous apprenez de la France de l'époque?

This offers scope, not only for teaching or reinforcing certain grammatical constructions which often present difficulties (e.g. *dont*, conditional tense, inversion of verb and subject), but also for imaginative language expansion (different adjectives, description and analysis of behaviour and attitudes, motive, disappointment of conventional expectations). Different language skills can also be developed, e.g. group discussion, individual analysis and research into other analagous situations. These can all then be written up into a review of the scene or indeed the film.

By this time students were asking for more general information on the major events of the Second World War in France. I used as an introduction the front page article from *Le Monde Dossiers Documents*, an issue which devoted a special feature to reprinted authentic documents from the contemporary French media. This issue proved to be an invaluable resource.

First, students were given the article, entitled *Les Français sous l'Occupation* (see p50). This text is demanding and I woiuld not expect them to grasp the details without careful reading and preparation as homework on their part. The article is also useful for giving the internal occupation boundaries within France, which allows disucssion of the precise political distincitions of the period and the differences or similarities between the occupied and so-called 'free' zones. Material such as this can be very fully supplemented by other relevant resource material on the period in *Thématique*, selected articles from the newspaper *Authentique*, as well as most course books such as *Au Point*.

The *Le Monde* article sketches out the policies of Pétain, why the French initially placed their confidence in him and why this confidence was so misplaced. Linguistically, it can be exploited in the following ways (see the questions below for concrete examples of the different grammatical or lexical items): synonyms, dictionary use and explanation in pupils' own words; unusual lexis; colloquial or idiomatic expressions; reinforcement of the passive voice; government of verbs.

Les Français sous l'Occupation

La 'drôle de guerre' (1939–1940) porte mal son nom. Elle sert de préface à la terrible défaite de juin 1940. Pour saisir l'ampleur de ce drame, vécu comme un traumatisme majeur par les Français, it faut toujours garder à l'esprit deux chiffres: à la signature de l'armistice entre l'armée française et la Wehrmacht, les trois cinquièmes du territoire national sont occupés par les nazis et 1,6 million de soldats bleu-blanc-rouge sont faits prisonniers. Bref, les Français, qui se croyaient invincibles, découvrent avec humiliation leur vulnérabilité.

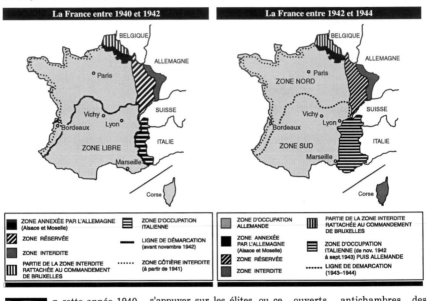

La France entre 1940 et 1942 — La France entre 1942 et 1944

En cette année 1940, la France ressemble à un cheval fourbu 'conduit par des cavaliers aveugles', selon la formule de Pierre Messmer. Déboussolés, jetés sur les routes de l'exode, les Français remettent leur destin entre les mains d'un vieux chef de guerre, Philippe Pétain, qui a tôt fait de s'emparer des 'pleins pouvoirs' à l'ombre de la tutelle allemande.

Le maréchal Pétain déclinera tout au long de L'Occupation une politique autoritaire dans laquelle on peut distinguer trois volets:
– la révolution nationale, qui, sous couvert de redonner à la France une colonne vertébrale, impose un ordre moral tout entier résumé dans le slogan vichyste 'Travail, famille, patrie' et l'hymne fredonné chaque jour par les écoliers: 'Maréchal, nous voilà ...'. Cette révolution-là tente de s'appuyer sur les élites, ou ce qu'il en reste, sur une presse muselée par la censure et des corps intermédiaires nommés par le régime;
– la collaboration, inaugurée dans l'espoir d'alléger les malheurs des Français, et qui conduit très vite à souligner l'impuissance national face aux diktats de Berlin. L'armée est contrainte au sommeil, la police commise aux basses œuvres, l'agriculture et l'industrie sommées de produire au profit de l'Allemagne;
– l'exclusion, qui illustre la volonté du régime de pourchasser ce qu'on appelle, à l'époque, les 'ennemis de l'intérieur'. Des lois organisent ainsi l'arrestation des francs-maçons, des communistes, des gaullistes et, de manière obsessionnelle, des juifs. L'historien Jean-Pierre Azéma a pu parler à juste titre d'un 'apartheid à la française'. Des camps d'internement sont ouverts, antichambres des camps de la mort situés en Allemagne et en Pologne.

Dans ce contexte, les résistants mirent longtemps à se regrouper, encore davantage à s'armer. Les Français, assommés par la propagande, tenaillés par la faim, plaçaient massivement leur espoir en la personne du maréchal Pétain avant de découvrir tardivement son rôle funeste. Ils étaient encore des centaines de milliers à l'applaudir dans la rue, en avril 1944, lors de ses déplacements.

A l'heure du bilan, lorsque les Français fêtèrent la liberté retrouvée, 600 000 d'entre eux avaient trouvé la mort durant ces années noires. L'appareil industriel était en loques. La France était à reconstruire.

Laurent Greilsamer

Le Monde Dossiers Documents:

Exploitation

Après avoir lu et preparé l'article, faites les exercises suivants:

1 Trouvez des synonymes pour les mots ou phrases suivants:

fourbu; sous couvert de; pourchasser; alléger; fredonner; la volonté; ainsi; à juste titre; deboussolé; avoir tôt fait de; sommé de

2 Expliquez dans vox propre mots ces expressions:

à l'ombre de la tutelle allemande; tenaillés par la faim; un rôle funeste; distinguer un volet; la basse œuvre; en loques; une presse muselée par la censure; remettre leur destin entre les mains de; décliner une politique; assommés par la propagande

3 Trouvez des examples du passif; du passé simple; des verbes qui gouvernent une préposition.

éreinté, épuisé; sous prétexte de; poursuivre, persécuter; réduire (et non pas illuminer ni eclairer); chantonner; le désir; de cette façon; avec raison, avec justesse; desorienté; ne pas tarder à; enjoint à

sous le contrôle ou la direction allemand/e; torturés par la faim; un rôle désastreux; voir trois aspects; les basses besognes; en lambeaux; une presse baillonnée par la censure; confier à la garde de; suivre, afficher; écrasés, accablés

mirent; la police commise; l'armée est contrainte; conduire à souligner; ressembler à; ôtre à; commettre à; mettre à

From the very wide-ranging selection of articles in the body of *Le Monde Dossiers Documents,* I chose to copy those which would allow maximum coverage of the major aspects of occupation. Below is the list, and the subjects which they represented, although in the interests of space only one is reprinted here: an account of the infamous *'Rafle du Vel' d'Hiv'.*

List of titles of articles

1 Itinéraire d'un chef de la Grande Guerre

2 Les juifs victimes de l'aryanisation

3 Les ordonnances allemandes en zone occupée

4 La rafle du Vel' d'Hiv'

5 Brasillach, journaliste collaborateur

6 Une nouvelle donne pour le cinéma

7 Les groupes francs, premiers mouvements de résistance

1 Potted biography of Petain which gives a historical context for defeatism

2 Information of the extent to which French Jews were dispossessed by their fellow countrymen; this can be linked to the current debate about restoration of stolen goods and money cp. Le Point 6 Dec 1997 'Revelations sur les archives francaises'

3 Revelations about the latent and overt anti-Semitism in France: the progressively harsher measures taken against Jews by the Vichy regime

4 The documented inhumanity of the French and German authorities in one infamous incident; statistics of deported Jews

5 Domination of the press by anti-Semitic and collaborationist sentiments; the role of writer as propagandist

6 Collaborationist tendencies in the cinema of occupied France: this can then be tied back in to the later Au revoir les enfants; *and* Lacombe Lucien.

7 Accounts of personal heroism; the brutality of the militia; and internecine rivalries between different types of Resistance movement.

La rafle du Vel' d'Hiv'

3 031 hommes, 5 802 femmes et 4 051 enfants raflés par la police française le 16 juillet 1942

L'aube du jeudi 16 juillet 1942 se lève sur l'un des épisodes les plus sombres de l'Occupation: la rafle du vel' d'Hiv'. Pendant deux jours, près de 4 500 fonctionnaires français de police, baptisés 'agents capteurs', arrêtent à partir de 4 heures du matin à leur domicile des familles juives: femmes jusqu'à cinquante-cinq ans, enfants à partir de deux ans et hommes jusqu'à soixante. Même les malades sont arrachés de leur lit d'hôpital. Après un premier regroupement dans les écoles de quartier ou dans les commissariats, ces files de 'prisonniers' qui ne sont coupables d'aucun délit sont dirigées vers des autobus à

plateforme. Les familles sont concentrées au Vélodrome d'Hiver (le 'Vel' d'Hiv''), rue Nélaton, dans le 15ᵉ arrondissement. On séparera les mères des enfants plus tard à coups de crosse, à l'abri des regards indiscrets, dans les camps du Loiret, de Pithiviers et de Beaune-la-Rolande. Quant aux célibataires et aux couples sans enfants, ils sont conduits directement à Drancy, et de là à Auschwitz.

La rafle a été soigneusement préparée par les SS Dannecker et Oberg d'un côté, René Bousquet, secrétaire général pour la police du ministère de l'intérieur de Vichy, Jean Legay, délégué de Bousquet en zone occupée, et Laval lui-même, de l'autre. Cependant, le bilan de l'opération est inférieur aux prévisions. Le

fichier mécanographique des juifs établi à la préfecture de police – récemment retrouvé – avait en effet laissé espérer aux Allemands comme à la police près de 25 000 arrestations. Au soir du 17 juillet: 12 884 personnes – 3 031 hommes, et surtout 5 802 femmes et 4 051 enfants – ont été appréhendées.

Rien n'a été prévu pour recevoir ces familles formées principalement de 'juifs apatrides'. (Allemands, Autrichiens, Polonais, Tchécoslovaques ou Russes), qui sont pour le moment les seuls à être arrêtés (parmi eux se trouvent cependant beaucoup d'enfants nés sur le sol français). L'avocat André Baur reconte: 'La vaste enceinte grouille de haut en bas ... Nous pénétrons sur la piste centrale par le tunnel. Une foule énorme dans les tribunes, où les fauteuils paraissent tous occupés ... De temps en temps, des jeunes gens apportent des baquets d'eau, et tous s'y précipitent pour remplir leurs quarts, leurs casseroles ou de simple boîtes de conserve. Sur la piste, à droite en sortant du tunnel, des brancards sont posés où geignent des femmes et des enfants étendus. Dans une petite enceinte à gauche, la Croix-Rouge a installé une ambulance où s'affairent les infirmières et les deux médecins. On a l'impression qu'il n'y a que des enfants et des malades. (...) Une femme devenue folle est liée sur un brancard, une autre a cherché à tuer son enfant avec une bouteille. Un autre enfant fut amené, les veines du poignet presque sectionnées par sa mère.'

Une lettre ecrité le 18 au Vel' d'Hiv' donne la mesure de la panique des internés: 'Nous sommes très malheureuses. A chaque instant il y a de nouveaux malades. Il y a des femmes enceintes, des aveugles ... Nous couchons par terre. ... Maman n'en peut plus. C'est encore plus ahurissant que toutes les femmes racontent des choses qui ne tiennent pas debout et, au lieu de se remonter, elles se descendent.' Parfois, sans raison, des applaudissements éclatent, et cessent presque aussitôt, témoignage du désarroi d'une masse en proie à un désespoir absolu.

Qui peut savoir pourtant du sort atroce qui attend cette foule ainsi parquée? L'inquiétude des internés fait constamment craindre aux autorités des réactions d'indiscipline ou des évasions. La rafle n'a-t-elle pas été marquée par quelques cas de suicide? La circulaire signée par le directeur de la police municipale Hennequin prescrit d'ailleurs aux 'agents capteurs' de procéder aux arrestations 'sans paroles inutiles et sans commentaires'. D'un autre côté, comment justifier aux yeux des futures victimes la fable de la déportation 'pour le travail', alors que ceux dont on se saisit sont en majorité des femmes, des enfants ou des vieillards inaptes à la moindre tâche? Ne libère-t-on pas du Vel' d'Hiv', justement, les 'juifs travailleurs', propres à servir de main d'œuvre aux autorités d'occupation?

En juillet 1942, la 'solution finale' fonctionne depuis près d'une année. Plus de 1 million de juifs sont morts. La presse anglosaxonne s'est faite l'écho de massacres et même du caractère systématique de l'entreprise de destruction nazie (à Londres, le *Jewish Chronicle*, dès janvier 1942, le *Daily Telegraph*, les 25 et 30 juin de la même année). Certes, ces nouvelles, parues dans des journaux britanniques, peuvent rappeler à Vichy le 'bourrage de crâne' dont les alliés s'étaient fait une spécialité durant le premier conflit mondial ...

© *Le Monde Dossiers Documents* 2/97

Each pupil was asked to choose an article 'blind': the old trick of photocopying them in different colours really does work! Once again, the subject matter of the matieral was largely unknown to them. Their project for the next three weeks (alongside more conventional 'A' level work) was to research their particular document, using all the resources available to them – in our case, libraries, CD-Roms, Internet, magazine and newspaper archives, radio and television, satellite broadcasts, oral history from families or friends – to prepare a version for discussion in their own words, in the target language, to the rest of the class. This exercise requires them to bring such skills as resumé, clear exposition of argument, discovery of illuminating backup documents and analysis of one or more points of view to bear, and has obvious potential for exploitation both as an oral or a written piece of work. It also means that they have to reply extempore to unexpected questions concerning both content and lexis. All of these skills correspond to current 'A' level language requirements and help to improve pupils' performance and confidence. This approach could also be used for essay, topic or course work; it is multifaceted and easily adaptable to a variety of different educational situations. When each student has finished his-her presentation, they are collated and handed out to the whole class, so that all students have quite a substantial core of a dossier on this period at their disposal.

At this point I introduced some other material of a more anecdotal and/or individual nature, to give a rounded, human dimension to the political and social tone of the articles. This can really help to bring home to them that these are the experiences of living human beings, not just pictures in a book or on a screen, and pupils do find them poignant and thought-provoking. Such material can be found in local histories available all over provincial France: there is a continuing market for this kind of account, and it is well worth while browsing in what appear to be unpromising stationers' shops, selling only the gutter press, faded postcards or babies' first readers, to uncover gems of first-hand archival material that you could never encounter in Britain. I used at this point two contradictory pieces of evidence, *Le chant du maquis de Bir Hakeim*, which can be used for further vocabulary extension, a discussion of the uses and abuses of propaganda, and its effectiveness, and inventories of names of deported Jews from the Charente, together with photographs of internment camp, e.g. Pithiviers, private family photos, and trains carrying French Jews to Drancy and the final solution. These make chilling reading.

To round off the dossier, and to show pupils how much they had learnt about the period since the start of the exercise, we finished with a clip, again from Louis Malle, this time from *Lacombe Lucien*: the scene in which Lucien is being measured by the Jewish tailor, Horn, for a pair of plus-fours paid for by his collaborator friend. Pupils were now familiar with the these of betrayal, complex relationships which cut across political divides, brutality and fear, collaboration and resistance. The scene served to reinforce their new-found knowledge as well as to show them how their grasp of language and their ability to manipulate it has improved.

Lastly, pupils were asked to evaluate what they had done and invited to say into what area of contemporary or historical France these researches would be likely to lead them. The verdict was unanimous, that this way of introducing them to more complex language structures and lexis was effective because of their engagement with the subject, and that it had improved reading, writing and oral skills imperceptibly, but enormously. They were themselves astonished at the amount of ground covered. Since then, this topic area and approach has been used by them to prepare oral topics on the Dreyfus case, the Papon trial, the question of Jewish gold and reparations, the establishment of the EU and the rise of Neo-Nazi groups in France.

From the teacher's point of view, the topic is open-ended and you learn as much as you teach. Initially a considerable amount of time is needed to collect suitable material, but this is amply rewarded by pupils' enthusiasm and the sense that they really have learnt to put their language learning into a European context which will stand them in good stead in the future.

Le Maquis charentais: 'Bir Hakeim' 1943–5

Le chant du Maquis de Bir Hakeim

Bravant la mort défiant les chaines
Nouse avons dit à l'ennemi
Enfants à la croix de Lorraine
A bas les traitres de Vichy

Nous disons non aux armistices
Toujours prêts nous n'avons qu'un cri
Victoire, Liberté, Justice
Toujours prêts et toujours unis

Assez mangé le pain des larmes
Chaque jour peut être Valmy
Prenons les bois, prenons les armes
Demain, demain, demain sourit

Seul aujourd'hui dans la nuit pleure
Le glas des morts et des bannis
Mais c'est demain que sonne l'heure
Des Te Deum pour le pays

Fini de nous cacher dans l'ombre
A mort les traitres à la Patrie
Sortons de nos forêts profondes
Attaquons partout l'ennemi

Et pour forger notre victoire
Dans les bois nos armes ont dit
Après la peine à nous la gloire
A nous toujours ceux du Maquis

La victoire ouvre la carrière
En avant les gars du Maquis
Debout jusqu'à l'heure dernière
Pour défendre notre Patrie

Chapter 6

Why do they do it? – An investigation into rates of participation and learner motivation in modern languages after GCSE and 'A' level

Keith Marshall

The increase in the participation in language learning in the education system has been at GCSE, where it is compulsory. Thereafter, when learners can decide for themselves, first in choosing 'A' levels and then university degrees, there is an alarming flight from languages. This is most marked in the area of specialist learning (single honours), but is also evident in the combination of languages with other disciplines, where entries are falling far behind those in HE as a whole. (See Appendix 1, p71, on 'Participation in language learning'.)

It is this worrying situation which prompted me to investigate what motivates learners when they choose whether to go on with languages. This study is concerned with the first key point of choice in the language learning cycle: the selection of 'A' levels. The decline at this point in the number of 'A' level linguists is the first manifestation that all is not well in the cycle of language learning. If we can understand better why they do it – why they continue with languages – and, more particularly, why they do not do it – why they turn their back on languages – then perhaps we can do something to halt the decline in language learning beyond GCSE. (See Appendix 2, p74, on the 'Methodology of the investigation'.)

Positive factors drawing learners to languages

Top ten positives

At the top of the positives (see Fig. 1, p57), *enjoyment of the subject* signifies a spontaneous response, different in essence from the more calculating implications of certain of the other factors. *Love of the language,* in third place, falls into the same category. It is remarkable that *Desire to travel,* in the life style aspiration category, should be so close to the top, but it is surely related to *Positive experiences of country and people* in fourth place. The other factors in the Top Ten Positives indicate broader academic ambitions (*Desire to combine a language with a humanities subject; Interest in its culture; Desire to be multi-lingual*) and an awareness of the languages and careers issue (*Perceived employment advantage; Desire to work abroad.*) It is worth remarking that, in the opinion of the teacher respondents, enjoyment of the subject, not the utilitarian consideration of better job prospects should be the top positive factor.

The importance of a *Positive response to communicative teaching* ties in with the most common positive factor 'written in' by respondents – the relationship between teacher and pupil, the effect on motivation of being well-taught in the classroom.

Figure 1

Why do students choose to continue language learning after GCSE and 'A' level?

Top ten positive factors
1 Enjoyment of the subject
2 Desire to travel
3 Love of language for itself
4 Positive experience of the country and people
5 Desire to be multi-lingual
6 Positive response to 'communicative' teaching
7 Desire to work abroad
8 Perceived employment advantage
9 Desire to combine a language with a humanities subject
10 Interest in its culture.

Degrees of positive influence: often or never? or somewhere in between?

The identification of a top-ten group of factors is helpful as a device for analysing learner motivation at the point of choosing whether to continue with languages. However, it must be acknowledged that quantitative differences separating and ordering the factors are not sufficiently distinct to allow us to say that the factor in, for example, fifth place is more frequently influential than the one in sixth place. In fact, the quantitative analysis, rather than producing a precise rank order, puts each factor on one of four levels of influence, according to whether it affects learner choice: **often/always, generally/often, sometimes/generally, sometimes/never** (see Fig. 2, p58).

While we should be careful of drawing over-ambitious conclusions from the fine detail of the rank order, Fig. 5 demonstrates a general consensus among the teacher respondents that only enjoyment of subject and desire to travel stand out as being more than generally influential. With the exception of *Enjoyment of subject,* the number of teachers who thought that any single factor (negative or positive) always applied, was rarely more than four and never exceeded twelve. The bulk of the rest are influential only sometimes or generally. In other words, these teachers see no decisively frequent factors influencing their pupils. The *Challenge of the subject* or *Interest in its culture* do not stand out as great motivating forces. It is, however, surely not without significance that *Desire to teach a language* is perceived by the teachers as almost never influencing the choice.

Figure 2

Why do students choose to continue language learning to 'A' level and beyond?
Positive factors: frequency of application

WHICH OFTEN/ALWAYS APPLY	
Enjoyment of subject	
WHICH GENERALLY/OFTEN APPLY	
Desire to travel	
WHICH SOMETIMES/GENERALLY APPLY	
Love of language itself	Challenge of subject
Positive experiences of country and people	Positive parent pressure
Desire to be multi-lingual	Positive response to 'target language
Positive response to 'communicative' teaching	only' in classroom
Desire to work abroad	Desire to study language(s) only
Perceived employment advantage	Desire to combine a language with
	science(s)/maths
Desire to combine a language with	Euro-enthusiasm at home
a humanities subject	Positive peer attitudes
Interest in its culture	Ease of subject
Desire to combine a language with	
a business course	
WHICH SOMETIMES/NEVER APPLY	
Desire to teach language	Euro-enthusiasm in the media
Desire to study its literature	Euro-enthusiasm among politicians

On the one hand, these findings regarding the positive factors are somewhat disappointing. To report that pupils carry on with languages principally because they enjoy the subject is not particularly enlightening. It begs more questions than it answers. Why do they enjoy the subject? On the other hand, some answers to that question begin to emerge from the responses to the other 22, more detailed, positive factors in the list.

Negative factors driving learners away from languages

Top ten negatives

While analysis of the responses regarding the positive factors influencing pupils succeeds to a limited extent in identifying strengths in the current experience of language learners which can be developed, it is among the negative ones that we must hope to find pointers to the weaknesses that need to be remedied.

Figure 3

Why do students choose not to continue language learning to 'A' level and beyond?

Top ten negative factors
1   Preference for other subjects
2   Languages are thought to be too difficult
3   Most students limited to 2 or 3 'A' level subjects
4   Lack of self-confidence in their language ability
5   Too big a leap from GCSE to 'A' level
6   Ignorance of benefits of language expertise
7   Constraints of 6th form timetable (e.g. languages timetabled against sciences)
8   Euro-scepticism among politicians
9   Euro-scepticism in media
10 Would have dropped languages earlier if allowed to

Once again we can usefully draw up a list of **Top ten factors** (see Fig. 3). Significantly, *Preference for other subjects,* at the top of the list, is the obverse of *Enjoyment of subject,* the number one factor in the Positive Top Ten. Deciphering the implications of it is problematic. On the surface it is a banality – one cannot imagine 6th formers opting for subjects which they do not prefer. Beneath that surface lies an unseen web of motivation as an explanation of why they prefer these other subjects. The gender imbalance in the language classrooms of many mixed comprehensives; the introduction of new vocational 'A' level subjects like Law, Media Studies and Psychology, seductively offering the chance to do something completely new; the greater readiness of girls to try out these new subjects as well as venture into the male domains in the physical sciences – these factors, amongst others, must make up the strands of this complex web motivating choices from which languages are increasingly excluded.

The other factors in the Negative Top Ten are dominated by the issue of aptitude and the degree of difficulty encountered (*Languages are thought to be too difficult* in second place, *Lack of self-confidence in their language ability* in fourth and *Too big a leap from GCSE to 'A' level* in fifth). Does this imply that other subjects are intrinsically easier and that that in part explains why pupils opt for them? There is considerable evidence that average 'A' level grades in some other subjects are higher. Pupils looking to go on to higher education may therefore conclude that these other subjects will provide a better route to a degree course, especially in a good university. On the other hand, the higher grades in other subjects could mean that modern languages are failing to appeal to the more gifted pupils, who are drawn to these other subjects, so raising the grade averages in them. It is also very possible that perception of difficulty on the part of learners may simply be a function of natural aptitude. Pupils who choose to do 'A' level French may well drop physics because they find it too difficult, just as for pupils who choose physics it is the reverse.

Curriculum and timetable constraints in the 6th form are also identified as disincentives (*Most students limited to two or three 'A' level subjects* and *languages timetabled against sciences*). The implication here is that some pupils are dropping languages in the 6th form because they have to, not because they want to. The teachers are saying that, if only there were a broader post-16 curriculum structure, which enabled pupils to do more subjects, they would choose to continue their language learning. There is the further possibility that language learning, already compulsory at Key Stages 3 and 4, should also be obligatory post-16.

The issue of languages and careers makes an appearance on the negative side (*Ignorance of the benefits of language expertise*). Teacher respondents feel that there is a good message on the professional advantages of language expertise that is not getting across. My own experience suggests strongly that this is indeed the case. In the eighteen months from February 1997 to July 1998 I visited some 70 schools across the UK, from Exeter to Glasgow and from Caernarfon to Dover, to talk to pupils from Year 9 upwards about the professional advantages of studying languages at 'A' level and beyond. It was a revelation to them to hear that:

- unemployment levels among language graduates in the mid-90's are lower than those of graduates in computer stud who go directly into jobs, only 5% go directly into teaching (mostly TEFL) and less than 1% become translators;
- 24% go into wholesale, retail or manufacturing companies, 19% into property, banking, business and finance, 12.8% into leisure transport and communications, 9.9% into public administration and social services, and 29% into a huge variety of other niches in the employment market;
- to get these jobs you do not have to combine a language with a 'vocational' subject – in some universities it is among the single honours language specialists that the unemployment rates are lowest (0% in some years among single French and single German graduates from Bangor);
- language graduates are beating those in nearly all other vocational and non-vocational subjects (except medicine and law) in the competition for jobs.

Not only are these messages failing to get across to pupils. So far as the hard statistical evidence is concerned, they are news to most modern language teachers and to a disturbingly large number of careers advisors. The myth of modern languages as an abstract academic subject which needs to be tied to a vocational subject, if it is to lead to anything other than teaching or translating, is widespread and deeply ingrained in the minds of the public and educational professionals. It needs a concerted effort by an army of well-informed language publicists to make the case for modern languages and blow the myth out of the water.

The data for this investigation was collected in the Spring of 1997, during the run-up to the General Election. The issue of Europe was part of the agenda of that election debate. Teacher respondents identified *Euro-scepticism among politicians and in the media* – part of the general category of wider social contexts influencing pupil choice – as a significant discouragement to pupils.

Degrees of negative influence – the key to understanding why they turn away?

As with the Top Ten Positives, the details of the order of the Top Ten Negatives should be treated with caution in discussion of what influenced choices most often. Once again, however, the quantitative analysis, while it does not create a precise rank order, puts each negative factor on one of four levels of influence, according to whether it affects learner choice often/always, generally/often, sometimes/generally, sometimes/never (see Fig. 4).

Figure 4

Why do students choose not to continue language learning to 'A' level and beyond?
Negative factors: frequency of application

WHICH OFTEN/ALWAYS APPLY
None
WHICH GENERALLY/OFTEN APPLY
Preference for other subjects Languages are thought to be too difficult Most students limited to 2 or 3 subjects at 'A' level Lack of self-confidence in own language ability
WHICH SOMETIMES/GENERALLY APPLY
Too big a leap from GCSE to 'A' level   Disappointment with GCSE Ignorance of the benefits of language expertise   experience Constraints of the 6th form timetable   Euro-scepticism at home (e.g. languages timetables against sciences)   Negative peer attitudes Euro-scepticism among politicians   Dislike of literature Euro-scepticism in media   Perceived irrelevance of Would have dropped MFL earlier if allowed to   languages to employment Fear of formal grammar teaching
WHICH SOMETIMES/NEVER APPLY
Negative parent pressure Insufficient intellectual challenge at GCSE Negative experience of a language's country and people Dislike of its culture Settling for an 'AS' language Unattractive 'A' level syllabuses Languages are thought to be too easy (89% of respondents thought this never applied)

Whereas there was one positive factor (*Enjoyment of subject*) on the often/always influential level, no negative factors were perceived as being that prevalent. On the other hand, five of the negative factors were reckoned to apply generally/often – four relating to aptitude and the difficulty of language learning and one to the constraint of being limited to two or three 'A' levels in the 6th form. As with the positives, the majority of the negatives are bunched on the sometimes/generally level, indicating that they play a limited but not frequent role in the learners' decision-making process. Not surprisingly, this level includes a mixture of factors: in the categories of personal aptitude (*Too big a leap from GCSE to 'A' level; Fear of formal grammar teaching*) broader social contexts (*Euro-scepticism among politicians in the media and at home; Negative peer attitudes*) and classroom experience (*Disappointment with GCSE; Dislike of literature*). In the middle of this group *Would have dropped languages earlier if allowed to* testifies to the presence of a certain number of pupils in the GCSE classes, and even at Key Stage 3, who are there against their will. And many of them probably *Perceive languages as irrelevant to their employment ambitions.*

The lowest level of influence (sometimes/never) is interesting for what it tells us about factors which the teachers think play little or no part in pupils' choice. The notion that languages are not attractive enough to bright pupils gets short shrift: *Insufficient intellectual challenge at GCSE*, and *Unattractive 'A' level syllabuses* are right down here at the bottom, all but ruled out as disincentives. Indeed, 89% of respondents reckoned no learner was ever put off because they thought that *Languages are thought to be too easy* – the most resounding negative response in the whole questionnaire. The presence on this level of *Settling for an 'AS' language* confirms the evidence from 'A' level Board entries: in the UK as a whole 'AS' languages have been a flop.

Even more than with the positive factors the analysis of the negatives has not turned up a clear set of overwhelmingly influential considerations which can be identified as the key to why so many turn their backs on languages. According to these teachers it is not the same one or two disincentives at the back of every decision to drop languages; learners decide to do so for many different reasons. Does this diversity of disincentives offer any possibility of remedial action? The predominant group – at the top of the table of negatives – of issues of aptitude and personal difficulty with languages, creates a certain scope for action. So, too, does the poor communication of the message on languages and careers, and, on the face of it, the constraints of the current 'A' level system. But the negative section of the questionnaire leaves many issues unresolved, on why pupils increasingly prefer other subjects.

Factors which can work both ways: contrasting pairs

In constructing the positive and negative sections of the questionnaire, pairs of motivating factors were created, allowing comparisons and contrasts to be made. This revealed some fascinating insights into how far certain factors operate in two directions, positively and negatively, on learner motivation (see Fig. 5).

On the related issues of the culture associated with a language and experience of the country and its people, it is clear that the positive effects far outweigh the negatives. The message from this must be that the more exposure learners can have to these aspects of language learning the better. Get them across the Channel on school trips, visits and exchanges. Teachers see little risk of turning them off, but every chance of enhancing their interest in the language.

Figure 5
Contrasting motivations

```
Interest in the culture  (27% often/always an influence)
                             v
Dislike of culture  (3.5% often/always an influence)

Positive experience of the country and people (33% often/always)
                             v
Negative experience of country and people (3% often/always)

Desire to study literature of  target language (5% often/always)
                             v
Dislike of literature (6% often/always)

Positive parent pressure (11% often always)
                             v
Negative parent pressure (10% often/always)

Positive peer attitudes (7% often/always)
                             v
Negative peer attitudes (13% often /always)

Desire to be multilingual (33% often/always)
                             v
Would have dropped subject earlier (18% often/always)

Euro-enthusiasm at home(18%), in media (11%), among politicians( 0%)
                             v
Euro-scepticism at home (13%), in media (15%), among politicians (16%)

Employment advantage (29% often/always)
                             v
Languages seen as irrelevant (14% often/always)
```

On the other hand, the hoary old chestnut of literature, so much an issue in the transition between 6th form and the old universities in the past, has ceased to register. No longer compulsory at 'A' level and easily avoided in the myriad variety of HE courses now available, only 5% of respondents thought it often or always a positive factor and 6 % a negative one.

Is it cool to be a linguist in the 6th form common room? What part do parents play? According to the teachers, parents are equally divided, but not very influential: 11% often/always positive and 10% negative. Peers, on the other hand, divide 7% to 13% between the positive and the negative. Again not dramatically influential, but peers are twice as likely to be discouraging as encouraging.

Contrasting personal attitudes to the acquisition of language skills emerged between those who were motivated by the desire to be multilingual (33% of respondents thought this was often or always an influence) and those who would have dropped the subject earlier if allowed to (18% often or always an influence). This relatively widespread ambition to excel in the essence of the subject is encouraging, but the presence of so many unwilling members of language classes must present pedagogical problems.

The twin issues of Euro-scepticism and Euro-enthusiasm are important in assessing the influence of wider social contexts on pupils' choices. Less than a fifth of the teacher respondents thought they often or always had an effect. However, it is interesting that, in the home, Euro-enthusiasm is thought to prevail (18% to 13%). The lead from the media, on the other hand, is, on balance, sceptical (15% to 11%), whereas politicians are seen as having a totally Euro-sceptic impact (16% to 0%). It is remarkable that not one teacher out of 289 thought that politicians often or always exerted a positive influence in this area! One wonders if the change of government since the collection of the data will have changed that perception.

On the utilitarian issue of languages and employment, while the relatively large proportion (29%) who see it as often or always positive offers limited reassurance, the 14 % of negatives is no worse than one might have expected as a reflection of the number of young people who intend to spend their entire working lives on this sceptered isle, remote from contact with foreigners.

Options for action: the teachers' prescription for improving language take-up

After examining the positive and negative factors influencing the decisions of pupils on whether to continue with languages, it should be possible to come up with suggestions for improving the take-up of languages at 'A' level and beyond. Eight areas for action were proposed:

- Reforms in Key Stages 3 and 4
- Reforms in provision for 16–18-year olds
- Innovations at primary level
- Recruiting, training and retaining good teachers
- More international links
- Better classroom resources
- Improved university courses
- Greater effort at national level

All the options for action, with four exceptions (each dealt with separately below) received positive support. The teachers were ready to see any plausible idea for improving language take-up given a chance. The interest lies in the variations in the degree of approval voiced for different suggestions, those receiving the highest approval ratings (Yes or Definitely Yes) standing out as the actions they would like to see prioritised, the ones on which resources and effort should be concentrated.

• Reforms in Key Stage 3 and 4

Two changes are called for at secondary level. The first is for smaller classes, endorsed by all but two respondents. If languages are to be taught effectively to a wide range of abilities, classes of thirty and more must be reduced. The second is that there should be more chances for pupils to do two modern languages. The thinking here seems to be that, while the physical sciences and the humanities have several separate subject slots on all school timetables, enabling pupils to specialise in these areas, the offer, all to frequently, of only one language slot makes it difficult for them to go on to develop the mental discipline of the specialist linguist.

By contrast, the option of abandoning compulsory modern languages for all in secondary schools, one of the four exceptions, was supported by only twelve respondents. Going back to the old days where languages were the preserve of an intellectual elite is decisively rejected. This old system may have produced proportionately more specialists. It might well make teachers' lives easier not to have to deal with the considerable number of unwilling participants in their classes. Nonetheless, these teachers do not want to solve the problem by retreating from the challenge of engaging the interest of all pupils in their subject. The effect on jobs might also have been a consideration of course! Another KS 3 and 4 suggestion is also rejected: greater encouragement of short courses.

• Reforms in provision for sixteen to eighteen-year olds

In the area of post-16 provision there is a call from a substantial minority (31%) for more attractive 'A' level syllabuses, with 40% thinking this would perhaps be a good idea. On the other hand a majority would like to see a change in the 6th form curriculum which make it more broadly based. While the reform of the 'A' level system under discussion looks like making slight moves in that direction, one of the options favoured by respondents to achieve this would be greater use of the International Baccalaureate. Languages are integral to this, and, in fact, 55% were positively (Yes or Definitely Yes) in favour of making a language compulsory in a new 'A' level system. More use of vocational qualifications in languages, presumably as an adjunct to 'A' levels, is also attractive and there is some support for a new one-year qualification to replace the current 'AS'.

• Innovations at primary level

The idea of giving children an earlier start on foreign languages by introducing them at primary school level, already adopted in Scotland, appealed to a large number of respondents (47% Yes or Definitely Yes), provided it was compulsory. There was substantial opposition to it if it were to be optional. Pupils arriving at secondary school with widely different levels of competence in a variety of languages would pose many problems of continuity.

• **Recruiting, training and retaining good teachers**

There is a widespread recognition that the shortage of language teachers is a serious problem. Attracting, training and retaining good teachers, particularly in German and Spanish, is a priority. How is this to be done? 56% went for the option of salary supplements for language teachers, but many called for better PGCE training (61%), more time and resources for INSET (78%), INSET in foreign countries (75%), training sabbaticals (77%). 81% want to see more foreign language assistants. In current conditions many schools do not feel they can devote money to employ supply teachers so that full-timers can have much more than a day or two per session for off-site INSET. And in the same cash-strapped schools accountants are all too often succumbing to the temptation not to replace language assistants at the end of their annual contracts. In too many parts of the UK the language assistant has recently become an extinct species.

• **Better classroom resources**

Better classroom resources is a familiar cry from schools generally. These teachers are no exception. 70–80% are asking for more technological equipment – satellite TV, interactive CD ROM's, e-mail, internet access. 73% want a relaxation of copyright restrictions on photocopying. The demand for more and better books comes slightly behind on 64%.

• **More international links**

Given the earlier recognition of the positive effect of exposure to the culture, the country and the people of the languages studied, one might have expected more international links to be a popular area for development. In the event, there is a certain scepticism about the value of town twinning and school trips. Images of town twinning associations dominated by the likes of Ambridge's Linda Snell and councillors junketing at the ratepayers expense seem to have had a damaging effect! Pupil exchanges are the favoured method of achieving that positive exposure.

• **Improved university courses and cooperation with schools**

Universities must have a vital role to play in any revival of language learning beyond GCSE. The teachers recommend a further reduction in the emphasis on single language degrees and the development of more joint degrees with other subjects, particularly the physical sciences, though universities which offer the latter already are hardly flooded with applications. On the issue of literature-based degrees, the pro's and anti's are, surprisingly, nearly equally balanced: 33% in favour of further de-emphasising literature, but 27% definitely against. But the single biggest contribution that the staff of universities can make, say the teachers, is to come down out of their ivory towers, forge links with schools and provide encouragement to pupils to carry on with their languages. Indeed, the present deepening crisis in recruitment to specialist university language departments means that the survival of many of them may depend on their taking such vigorous action.

- **Greater effort at national level**

Engaged as they are in the exhausting daily routines of the classroom, these teachers have not lost sight of the larger context within which they are struggling to do their job. In fact their loudest demand of all is for leaders in industry and politics to adopt more positive attitudes. They call for a national strategy to promote language expertise and develop language-learning in the UK. This requires politicians to recognise the damage that they have caused by their Eurosceptic cynicism. It requires government and industry to give a lead to teachers and learners by communicating to young people particularly the benefits to them and to the country of expertise in languages. The list of Top Ten Options for Action puts these demands way out ahead of all others – ahead even of the need for smaller classes (see Fig. 6).

Figure 6

What can we do to improve take-up in language learning at 'A' level and beyond?

Top ten options for action
1 More positive attitudes in industry
2 More positive political approach to Europe.
3 Better communication of benefits of language learning
4 Smaller classes at KS 3 and 4
5 More teachers of Spanish
6 More teachers of German
7 More foreign language assistants
8 A comprehensive National Language Strategy
9 More time and resources for INSET
10 equal (a) More chances to do two foreign languages.
(b) Pupil exchanges with schools in other countries.

The overall message from the teachers

While there are many similarities, recurring themes running through the responses from different parts of the country on what influences pupils' choices in relation to languages, there is some evidence of divergence between different kinds of schools and colleges. Teachers in grant-maintained and LEA-supported schools presented broadly similar perceptions of their situation: marginally optimistic overall, with a slightly greater frequency of positive rather than negative factors at work. FE and 6th form colleges were, by comparison, consistently more aware of the negative factors, except in the area of languages and careers where they reported more positive learner perceptions than any other respondents. However, the most up-beat message, particularly with regard to the spontaneous personal response of pupils to language learning, came from the independent schools. One suspects that this has something to do with better resources, smaller class sizes and the selectivity of intake, but the numbers of pupils going on with languages in many of the independent schools which responded was higher, as a proportion of their 6th forms, than in the rest. This seems to suggest that, within these schools, languages are holding their own more successfully against other subjects. Single sex schools also seemed to present more vigorous language participation, and many of these were independent.

Though not all blessed with the advantages of those in the independent sector, the general picture painted by the 289 teachers who responded is one of KS 3 and 4 language classrooms where, if they have rather too many pupils and not enough teachers, if they could do with some more classroom resources, and a bit more access to modern technologies, the pedagogy has got it about right. Most of the respondents say they see more of their pupils reacting positively than negatively to the intellectually satisfying challenge of language learning; to the experience of the language classroom; to the exposure to the other cultures, countries and peoples; to the demands made on them by GCSE and the prospect of the 'A' level syllabuses currently on offer; to the professional advantages they expect to derive from language skills. Those who are deterred give up because languages are just too difficult for them; because government and industry are not pulling their weight; or because they may want to do languages, but the narrow 'A' level system won't let them.

This not altogether gloomy picture sits ill with the crisis which prompted this investigation: the alarming reversal, over the last five years, in the numbers doing 'A' level languages and going on to university language courses. So far as these teachers are concerned, the causes of this are located mostly elsewhere, with politicians and businessmen. And the solutions must come from the efforts and initiatives in institutions outside their own – primary schools, universities, government. These solutions – more secondary teachers and language assistants, primary language teaching, a broader 6th form curriculum – will all cost money. And the people who must decide that money is to be spent are not the language teachers.

Yet is there perhaps not more to it than that? There are certainly some flies in the ointment. If languages are difficult, they always have been. It is not the sudden discovery of their difficulty that is driving pupils away. Besides, students have flocked to study English in ever-increasing numbers over the last five years (see Fig. 8, p73), without government and industry mounting campaigns in favour of the subject. On the other hand, vigorous campaigns, in schools and colleges, by the engineering profession and the London

Mathematical Society and their academic supporters, have done little to reverse the decline in numbers in maths and engineering. Are UK university language departments destined to go the same way as those in US university language departments, where 85% of the students are only doing languages for non-specialist courses? Furthermore, if English and Welsh 6th forms are too narrow, those asking for reform must explain why the long-established Scottish system of five highers has seen the numbers opting for Higher Grade languages drop even more than the numbers doing 'A' levels in the rest of the UK. And to cap it all, comparisons between secondary pupils' attitudes to their school subjects in the 70s and the 90s seem to show that, while most subjects are about the same, now as then, the children simply don't like languages nearly as much as they used to.

The questionnaire as presented – the factors proposed as explanations for why some pupils choose to go on and others don't, the options for action suggested – succeeded in throwing light on some of the main issues involved in the motivation of language students. It has made some progress towards establishing which factors are most and least often influential in choices made by these pupils. The opinions analysed and quantified are authoritative. They came from a representative sample of the most experienced professionals in the field: secondary language teachers. But their perceptions of their pupils constitute only one perspective on the issue. And those perceptions have raised enough further questions to justify broadening the investigation. CILT made this initial investigation possible with a contribution to the cost and have provided platforms for disseminating the results. Again with CILT's help, a further investigation is now underway, this time of the perceptions of a selection of the pupils themselves, both those who are going on with languages beyond GCSE and those who have decided not to. The pupils perceptions of their own motivation, placed alongside those of the teachers, should help to clarify some of the questions raised in this first stage.

What future for languages beyond GCSE?

Worst case scenario

At worst, the future for the serious learning of modern languages in the UK is bleak. If we just cross our fingers and hope for things to get better, the danger is that the decline in 'A' level entries and in admissions to specialist university language courses will continue. The supply of expert linguists will gradually dry up, creating a crippling shortage of qualified teachers. Languages will have be dropped from the compulsory core of the curriculum at Key Stages 3 and 4 and will slip to the margins of 6th form and higher education. A certain tradition of insular pride in parts of the British establishment, along with a perception that English is becoming the world language and 'everyone else out there is learning it (aren't they?)' could provide a complacent rationale for allowing this to happen.

Best case scenario: a strategy for revival

But this alarming scenario is by no means inevitable. We may not yet understand completely all the reasons why more pupils in recent years have been choosing not to continue with languages at 'A' level and beyond, but this does not mean we cannot take counter-measures that have a reasonable chance of success.

We must continue to develop the auxiliary service role of language teaching, for it is vital that a reasonable proportion of people in every sector of the British workforce should be able to do their job, in part, through other languages. The extent and the nature of the language and cultural knowledge needed will vary. But to develop the knowledge to whatever level will require well motivated professionals with linguistic and teaching expertise.

More importantly, we must sustain the vitality of modern languages as a subject of learning in its own right. Without this, the quality of the learning offered in the subject will decline, undermining not only the utilitarian mission of languages as an auxiliary service, but also their unique role in the development of civilisation and understanding among different language groups.

The present investigation has not found all the answers, but any revival strategy must seek to make the profession of teaching languages and the experience of learning them more effective and attractive. That strategy would have to include our providing, as a priority, the necessary means for recruiting more well-trained teachers and native language assistants, smaller classes, enhanced international school links. The argument for broadening the 6th form curriculum is not exclusively a languages issue by any means. Surely, as part of a multi-disciplinary reform, it is worth creating greater chances of doing languages in the hope that other measures will improve the intrinsic motivation of learners.

The teachers who contributed to this investigation were deeply convinced that government and industry must give a lead, that this would transform the climate, would make people of all ages take languages seriously. Since the teachers expressed this view so strongly, the Government and the Nuffield Foundation have set up an enquiry into the present state and future development of foreign languages in the UK. This action and the helpful publicity it has attracted in all sections of the public media and specialised language publications is most encouraging. It gives those of us who sustain foreign languages by teaching them and those who can do so by using them beneficially an opportunity to collaborate in charting the future of languages in the UK. It is our responsibility to see that this opportunity is not wasted, by helping the Nuffield Inquiry into Languages to get to the heart of the matter and rally support behind an imaginative and workable National Language Strategy.

Appendix 1: Participation in language learning

Trends in secondary schools

More people are learning a foreign language in Britain today than at any time in the past. Some of these learners are doing it for pleasure through adult education classes. Others are employees doing it for the benefit of their companies. But the great bulk of these learners are secondary school pupils, doing it because in most of Britain a modern foreign language is a compulsory part of the national curriculum at Key Stages 3 and 4.

Figure 7

**Trends in specialist language learning
in secondary schools in the UK**

ENTRIES FOR GCSE IN THE UK

	1990	1995	% increase
French	281,576	350,027	+24.3%
German	84,306	129,386	+53.5%
Spanish	24,872	40,762	+63.9%

ENTRIES FOR 'A' LEVEL IN THE UK

	1992	1997	% change
French	31,261	25,881	-17.2%
German	11,338	10,440	-7.9%
Spanish	4,720	5,606	+18.8%

PERCENTAGE OF GCSE CANDIDATES CONTINUING TO 'A' LEVEL

	% of 1990 GCSE candidates continuing to a 'A' level	% of 1995 GCSE candidates continuing to a 'A' level	Decrease (1990–95) in % of GCSE candidates continuing to 'A' level
French	11.1%	7.4%	-33.3%
German	13.4%	8.1%	-39.6%
Spanish	19.0%	13.8%	-27.4%

Data from QCA

GCSEs in modern languages are one of the great success stories of the National Curriculum. Between 1990 and 1995 (see Fig.7) the numbers doing GCSE French increased by almost a quarter, those doing German by more than a half and those doing Spanish by more the 60%. This represents a triumph for all of those who argued that languages could and should be made accessible to pupils to whom they had previously been, effectively, denied. It is a credit to teachers who pioneered languages for lower ability groups, to exam boards who devised radically new syllabuses and to publishers and authors who produced innovative learning materials. The enormous increases for German and Spanish testify to the success of the policy of diversifying the languages taught in schools. While French continues to dominate largely because of the skills of the existing language teachers, the majority of pupils now have the possibility of studying another language, either instead of or in addition to French.

It was the expectation of the prophets of this language learning revolution that it would be continued in the later stages of the education system. Indeed, for a number of years in the late 80s and early 90s the numbers doing language 'A' levels and going on to degrees involving languages increased. Once again, bold innovations played an important part in the form of new syllabuses and fresh learning materials at 'A' level and a great increase in the number and range of degree courses, particularly in the new universities. This was all in the context of important increases in the proportion of 16-year-olds opting to stay on in education through the 6th form and beyond.

But, while the numbers doing GCSE have more than held up, since 1992 entries for 'A' level languages and applications for university courses involving languages have begun to fall.

Figure 1 shows the dramatic difference, over five-year periods, between the numbers of those doing GCSE's and those doing 'A' levels in languages. In French, a 24.3% increase at GCSE contrasted by 17.2% falls at 'A' level. In German, a 53% increase at GCSE contrasted by a 7.9% fall at 'A' level. Only in Spanish is there an increase at 'A' level – 18.8%

Figure 1 also demonstrates the decline in the continuation rates between the GCSE generations of 1990 and 1995. Whereas 11.1 % of the 1990 GCSE generation went on to pass 'A' level French in 1992, only 7.4% of the 1995 generation did so. In German the equivalent decline was from 13.4% to 8.1%. And even in Spanish the proportion of those continuing went down, from 19.0% to 13.8%. In other words the proportion of pupils continuing with a language after GCSE to 'A' level dropped, over five years, by a third in French (33.3%), and by rather more in German (39.6%). Even in Spanish, although the number of 'A' level passes is up, as a proportion of the GCSE numbers it is down by 27%. This trajectory is very alarming.

Trends in universities

At the next key point in the language learning cycle, entry to university, the picture is again one of declining participation, both in absolute numbers and in the proportion of those with 'A' level passes going on to do degrees (see Fig.8).

The decline in absolute numbers is to be expected, as a knock-on effect from the decline in 'A' level passes. Over the seven years between 1990 and 1997, this decline is steepest in the entry to single honours degrees: French (16.3%), German (33.%) and Spanish (22.3%).

Figure 8

Trends in universities

ADMISSIONS TO HE COURSES IN THE UK

Courses	1990	1997	% change
Single Honours French	1183	990	-16.3%
Single Honours German	528	354	-33.0%
Single Honours Spanish	300	243	-22.3%
Jt & Comb Degrees (incl Eng.)	5741	7338	+27.8%
Single Honours English	4410	7621	+72. 8%
All HE courses	191022	336338	+76.1%

PERCENTAGE OF 'A' LEVEL PASSES CONTINUING TO SINGLE HONOURS DEGREES

	% of 1990 'A' level passes continuing to Single Hons degrees	% of 1997 'A' level passes continuing to Single Hons degrees	Decrease (1990–97) in % of 'A' level passes continuing to Single Hons degrees
French	4.3%	3.8%	11.6%
German	5.6%	3.4%	-39.0%
Spanish	7.8%	4.3%	44.9%

ADMISSIONS TO JOINT HONOURS DEGREES

Courses	1995	1997	% change
Jt language degrees	2754	2696	-2.1%
Jt languages with non-language subjects	10114	10586	+4.7%
All HE courses	290596	336338	+15.7%

Data from UCAS

What is more worrying is the drop in the proportion of 'A' level students going on to university. The drop in French is significant (from 4.3% of 'A' level passes in 1990 to 3.8% in 1997): down 11.6%. In German it is much worse (from 5.6% of 'A' level passes in 1990 to 3.4% in 1997): down 39%. It is worst of all in Spanish (from 7.8% of 'A' level passes in 1990 to 4.3% in 1997): down 44.9%. Another alarming trajectory in specialist language learning.

It is often said that students are turning away from the narrow specialism of single honours and opting for joint honours programmes, either with another language or with a non-language. There is some truth in this. Unfortunately, data from the early 90's does not allow us to separate off joint honours foreign language entries to universities. Between 1995 and 1997, however, the number of entries to joint language courses went down by 2.1%. Over the same short period, those combining languages with other subjects went up by 4.7%, an increase largely accounted for by a rise in the number of non-UK students on such courses.

Put in the context of an overall rise of 76.1% in the number of entries to all university first degree courses between 1990 and 1997, the decline in single honours entries is shocking, particularly if put alongside, for example, the rise in entries to Single Honours English of 72.8%. The stagnant level of joint honours entries is nothing like so bad, but still very poor by comparison with the dramatic increase of three quarters in HE participation as a whole.

Appendix 2: Methodology of the investigation

Questionnaire addressed to secondary teachers

The study approached these questions of motivation by drawing on the experience of established secondary and FE language teachers. A questionnaire was sent out to the heads of modern languages departments in schools and colleges in the UK and to some anglophone schools abroad. It was divided into three sections:

- Positive factors affecting student choice
- Negative factors
- Options for action to improve take-up.

In all, 289 responses were received (see Figs. 9 and 10). They constituted a representative cross-section of UK schools and colleges, both in terms of their location in the different countries and their educational status, within and outside the state sector.

The positive section of the questionnaire presented a list of 25 possible factors and the negative section 24. Respondents were invited to tick boxes indicating, from their experience, how far each of these factors affected students, when they decided whether to continue or not with a modern language beyond GCSE. Respondents could grade their responses on a scale from Don't know, through

Never, Sometimes, Generally, and Often to Always. A blank box was also offered at the end of each section inviting respondents to write in factors not on the lists.

Figure 9

Questionnaire returns: Type of school/college

Local Education Authority	140
Independent	51
FE/6th Form Colleges	48
Grant Maintained	46
Miscellaneous	4
Total	289

Figure 10

Questionnaire returns: Countries

England	234
Wales	29
Scotland	19
Northern Ireland	5
Channel Islands	1
Belgium	1
Total	289

Quantifying the responses

To quantify the responses in the 289 questionnaires returned, numerical values were attributed to the list of possible answers (Don't know 0/ Sometimes 1/ Generally 3/ Often 4/ Always 5).

The relative importance of individual factors within each section (positive and negative) were determined by weighted average of all responses (max 289) to each question.

Section 3 presented 51 options for action, divide into 8 sub-sections. Again respondents were asked to tick boxes, this time to indicate how far they supported each option for action. A range of possible degrees of approval was again offered and quantified numerically (Don't know 0/ Definitely no -2/ No -1/ Perhaps + 1/ Yes + 2/ Definitely yes +3). The degree of overall support for or opposition to individual options for action was again determined by weighted average of all responses (max 289) to each question.

In looking at the standard errors associated with each weighted average, the standard error of the difference between two weighted averages was approximated, using a 5% significance level for the test.

It should also be borne in mind that, in examining the positive and negative influences, the questionnaire seeks to establish how often they affect learners' decisions whether to continue languages, not their importance.

The factors proposed as motivating the learners' decision to continue or not fell into a variety of categories:

- the spontaneous response to the experience of language learning
- language learning as a classroom experience
- in-country experience of languages learned
- aptitude and the degree of difficulty encountered
- broader academic ambitions
- curriculum and timetable constraints
- life-style aspirations associated with a knowledge languages
- languages and careers
- personal and wider social contexts

These verbal categories of motivation are helpful in interpreting the rank order of individual positive and negative factors produced by the quantitative analysis, both for the information they provide and for the questions they pose.

Epilogue

The new 'AS' and 'A' levels

Glenis Shaw

The new specifications for Advanced level GCEs which will be available from September 2000 offer a course made up of six modules; three to be taken in the first year after GCSE and a further three to be taken in the following year. This does not preclude all six from being taken at the end of the two-year course if wished. The Advanced level specifications are available from the examination boards for use from September 2000.

What effect will the new 'AS' and 'A' level examinations have on modern foreign languages? Participants at our conference were overwhelmingly in favour of the then new proposals. These included the idea that some students should take five 'AS' levels in the first year and continue with three 'A' level subjects in their second year of study. The 'S' in 'AS' now stands for subsidiary. 'AS' can be taken after one year of further study from GCSE because it is not as advanced as, but on the way to, an award at 'A' level. This was seen as an opportunity to increase those numbers of students taking 'AS' level and to capture those who now, for example, specialise in science. There was a firm belief that many would opt to continue with their language learning, having completed and succeeded at 'AS' level. In the meantime some schools have also seen that this is ideal for accelerated classes where GCSE is taken early and an 'AS' level examination can be offered which ensures a higher intellectual challenge and greater motivation for students to continue further in their study of a modern foreign language.

Below is an outline of the new subject criteria for modern foreign languages for the GCE Advanced Subsidiary and Advanced Level specifications.

Aims

'AS' and 'A' level specifications in modern foreign languages should encourage students to:

- develop understanding of the spoken and written forms of the modern foreign language from a variety of registers;
- communicate confidently, clearly and effectively in the modern foreign language through both the spoken and written word, using increasingly accurate, complex and varied language;

- increase their sensitivity to language and language learning;
- develop critical insights into, and contact with, the contemporary society, cultural background and heritage of countries and communities where the modern foreign language is spoken;
- develop positive attitudes to modern foreign language learning.

Main points of the specification

- 'AS' is a subset of the 'A' level specification;
- There are 6 modules of which 3 are at 'AS' level and 3 at A2 level. (All 6 modules may be taken together at the end of 2 years.);
- Students should normally have acquired the skills, knowledge and understanding equivalent to those specified for GCSE at Higher tier in the relevant language;
- Specifications may have a maximum internal assessment weighting of 30%. Not more than 20% may be located in the 'AS' or the A2;
- Assessment should include a minimum of 20% synoptic assessment taken at the end of the course and externally assessed;
- No dictionaries will be allowed in any external assessment;
- A maximum of 10% of the total marks for the subject at each level may be awarded for answers in English, Welsh or Irish;
- Specifications in modern foreign languages should provide opportunities for developing and generating evidence for assessing the key skills of communication, Information technology, improving own learning and performance and working with others;
- The four assessment objectives are weighted differently at 'AS' and 'A' level. They are:
  AO1 – understand and respond, in speech and writing, to spoken language.
  AO2 – understand and respond, in speech and writing, to written language.
  AO3 – show knowledge of and apply accurately the grammar and syntax prescribed in the specification.
  AO4 – demonstrate knowledge and understanding of aspects of the chosen society.
- The specifications include grade descriptions for Grade A, C and E at 'A' level (but not at 'AS' level);
- Appendix 1 of the criteria contains a list of grammar and structures in the target language for 'AS' and 'A' level.

The new examinations may well have different assessment objectives. Teachers need not be afraid. They will need to ask the question: 'How do I need to change what I am teaching at the moment?' They may wish to update, reassess and realign their resources for teaching, but this is a process that teachers go through continually. Good 'A' level teaching will continue to produce successful 'A' level students, achieving their full potential. Let us hope there will be a greater number of them!

Documentation

Qualifications 16–19. A guide to the changes resulting from the Qualifying for Success consultation.

GCE Advanced Subsidiary (AS) and Advanced level specifications. Subject criteria for modern foreign languages.

Curriculum 2000: Implementation of the 16–19 curriculum, QCA, 1999

The above documents can be obtained from: QCA Publications, PO Box 99, Sudbury, Suffolk CO10 6SN Tel: 01787 884 444; fax: 01787 312950

GCE 'A' and 'AS' level modern languages specifications can be obtained from:

OCR Publications: OCR, Mill Wharf, Mill Street, Birmingham B6 4BU; Tel: 0121359 2913

AQA Publications Department, Stag Hill House, Guildford, Surrey GU2 5XJ or Aldon House, 39, Heald Grove, Rusholme, Manchester M14 4PB

Edexcel Publications, Bellamy Road, Mansfield, Notts. NG18 4LN

Learning to succeed: a new framework for post-16 learning, DfEE, 1999, The Publications Centre, PO Box 276, London SW8 5DT; Tel 0345 02 34 74

N.B. All the above organisations' documents can be found on the Internet.